The Meaning of Fishing

Member Stories & Tips

Minnetonka, Minnesota

The Meaning of Fishing
Member Stories & Tips

Printed in 2011.

Tom Carpenter
Creative Director

Jenya Prosmitsky
Book Production & Design

Michele Teigen
Senior Book Development Coordinator

Laura Holle
Book Development Assistant

Mike Hehner
Tip Editor

Bill Lindner Photography
Mark Emery
Doug Stamm
Photographers

The Green Agency
Cover Image

Bill Reynolds
Illustrator

A special thanks to all the members who submitted stories, tips, recipes, photos and illustrations.

6 7 8 9 / 15 14 13 12 11

ISBN 10: 1-58159-147-0
ISBN 13: 978-1-58159-147-7
© 2002 North American Fishing Club

North American Fishing Club
12301 Whitewater Drive
Minnetonka, MN 55343
www.fishingclub.com

Contents

Introduction

Midnight. The boat is safe and sound in its place in the garage. All our fishing gear is stowed away until our next outing, probably in a week at most. My boys are sleeping soundly in their beds. The one fish I let them keep is filleted and in the freezer. I am finally lying down too, and I realize I must be falling asleep with a smile on my face:

The big, orange, cigar-shaped bobber actually makes a violent "whoosh" noise against the water as a big fish hits the sucker minnow dangling 8 feet below. I grab the rod, feed some line, then turn on the trolling motor and follow the orange beacon travelling erratically below the brown-stained water of this St. Croix River backwater. My knees shake and the boys sense a tremble in my voice.

Finally the bobber stops and I reel up the slack, feel the rod load, and set the hook with one big sweep from the hips. This is a big fish! I hand the rod to Jeremiah, hold-

ing on with one hand in case he decides to drop it when he sees what's on the other end. But the 8-year-old fights the fish with determination. Ethan holds the net and I think, what the heck, let him try it.

The pike tires after a couple minutes, and with one stroke the 6-year-old nets the fish head-first, perfectly. Then we all fall backwards in a heap, the pike thrashing madly about the boat and causing a general and slimy ruckus. After admiring her and taking a couple pictures, we put her back, never having measured her but knowing she was big and old enough to deserve to live. She darts back down into the brown depths, and we have a memory to last forever.

No matter how long or how hard we fish, the effort is always worth it. That's quite evident in the NAFC member stories in this book, *The Meaning of Fishing.* Here are stories of big fish (of course), little fish, many fish, no fish, adventures big and small, the magical places we go to fish … and also people (those with us and those gone now to better fishing grounds) that we love, and love to fish with.

As you'll see, there are many meanings to fishing. But in the end I contend that they all roll up into one simple category: Memories. They remain etched on our mind's eye to help us whether times are good or bad or hectic or slow or happy or sad. It is fishing memories—and the anticipation of creating new ones—that helps carry us through life.

We at the NAFC are proud to be able to share these special stories. May they bring you entertainment and joy. You may even pick up a few ideas for fishing success. But most of all, may these tales and tips help you recall the meaning of fishing—the memories that stay with us in those carefree moments between "awake" and "asleep," when what makes you very happy is so simple and clear.

Tom Carpenter
Editor—North American Fishing Club Books

ut after 50 years, that memory still remains as sharp as if it happened this afternoon. It is the foundation on which a lifelong passion is built. Every kid needs a memory like that. One so powerful that it can transform an old man's heart into that of a little boy, every time he gets on the water.

—From "Hooked for Life"

Just Fishing

In Memory of Grandpa

When I was young I never thought that growing up near the banks of Lost Creek would impact my life so much in later years. It is just a small creek, growing smaller as each year passes. There used to be many different species of fish that lived in the waters of Lost Creek—catfish, goggle eye, bass and perch, just to name a few.

When I was a young girl, it was my grandpa who first put a fishing pole in my hand. He was an avid hunter and fisherman back when hunting and fishing were a means to put food on the table or you went without. I remember when he'd be out in the yard putting new line on his reel and making sure his equipment was in top working order. I thought I was so special when he'd put a stick through the hole in the line spool and tell me to walk away a few steps. He'd start turning the crank and the line would swish as the spool spun on the stick.

At some point, he put a lead sinker on the end of the line and let me practice casting. I guess it was at that time that my love for fishing was planted. Living so near the creek, he would take me with him on little fishing expeditions. With fishing pole in hand we would walk down the hill to the creek and begin by fishing near the little dam that spanned the stream. This was where the deepest hole was; it was also the swimming hole. No fishing there when people were swimming. We would usually walk upstream and try out any little hole of water.

There were many tree limbs waiting to snag my bait. I say bait because he very rarely let me fish with his lures. He knew I would get them hooked in a tree and probably lose them. He would never get mad or upset no matter how many times I got my hook stuck up in the trees. He would patiently take my pole and work the hook free when possible. My grandpa must have been the most patient man in the world. I can still remember the thrill of catching even a small fish—the same thrill I get today when I feel that tug on the end of the line. I would not have had all these memories and my love for fishing if it hadn't been for my grandpa. It wasn't very many years

ago that my grandpa passed away. Since I am the only member of my family who enjoys fishing, I was given all his fishing tackle and the pole he had in the back of his truck when he died.

Of course, these days I fish at the nearby lake. Unfortunately, it's hardly possible to fish on Lost Creek anymore. Now it's all owned by private landowners who don't particularly like people walking up and down the creek. It doesn't really matter, since there are hardly any fish left anymore. The saddest thing of all is that just last month a train collision on a trestle that crosses this wonderful little stream poured oil and diesel into the water, killing fishes, frogs, crawdads and many other wildlife species. Who knows how long it will take for the stream to cleanse itself of those impurities.

Evelyn Proctor
Seneca, Missouri

To Fish... or Not to Fish?

You're an avid angler. You prize your time on the water. You enjoy fishing and you appreciate every fish you catch. Sometimes you seek the solitude of fishing alone. More often, you experience angling adventures with a buddy. But, every now and then, you want to share a fishing trip with your wife or girlfriend. However, if you're like me, there's just one problem—your "best ever" catch doesn't like to catch! I hope my tale will reveal ideas you can use to resolve this dilemma.

Although my wife, Tinsley, had enjoyed many activities with me over the years, fishing was not one of them. Tinsley did not want to fish; did not like to fish; in fact, refused to fish! Recently, however, I was at long last able to persuade her to accompany me on a "fishing" trip by promising to do some things differently than I normally would.

Fortunately, our appointed day for the "fishing" trip dawned with the promise of perfect weather—sunshine, low humidity, zero chance of rain, refreshing breeze. While I hitched up the boat, Tinsley prepared a picnic lunch. By mid-morning we were on our way to Caesar Creek Lake.

Between "arrive late and leave early" we had a great time. After launching the boat, we first spent some time just cruising around the lake. Tinsley liked to drive the boat, and I like to explore possible future fishing spots. After a restroom break at the dock, we headed for a tree-lined cove, tied up in the shade, and enjoyed our picnic lunch. After lunch, while I fished, my wife read a couple chapters in her book, worked a cross-stitch and even took a nap.

Fishing that day was as simple as it gets, short of a cane pole and bobber. Cast toward a stick-up, let the bait sink awhile, reel in slowly, every so often, then "fish on!" The catch for the day, five small fish, was nothing to brag about, but this day was about much more than numbers or size.

Mid-afternoon found us headed home with the lasting memory of pleasant time shared on the water. We both look forward to another outing.

So, take heart, fellow anglers with non-fishing partners. By making a few adjustments to your usual *modus operandi*, you may be able to persuade your sweetheart to join you in the boat as I did. And, who knows? Maybe someday she'll ask to borrow your fishing rod! Just remember, whether or not she actually fishes, sharing pleasant times on the water may help keep your "catch of a lifetime" from becoming the "one that got away." Here are the secrets:

• Pick a nice-weather day. Don't make her "fish" in the cold or rain.

• Provide comfortable seating. No "bench" seats for the lady.

• Take restroom breaks as needed. You'll both feel better.

• Encourage your honey to read, drive the boat, sew, or do whatever she enjoys doing. You catch the fish.

• Take it easy. Do your intense fishing at those times when she's not along.

• Limit your time on the water. Save the "dawn to dusk" outing for a trip with your buddy.

Patrick Richter
Dayton, Ohio

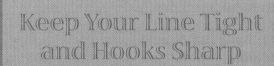

Keep Your Line Tight and Hooks Sharp

Figure eight after each cast, no matter what. If you become good friends with lure manufacturers, do some experimenting. Don't be afraid to try something different. Put rubber worms on bucktails to entice strikes.

A. Jim Heffner
Brodhead, Wisconsin

Hooked for Life

The world of 1951 was a very different place from the one we live in today. The broadcast media was mostly AM radio. A selection of recorded music came in a book, like a photo album, containing a collection of rigid Bakelite 78 rpm platters (one tune per side). Air travel was just starting to become competitive with the streamlined passenger trains that epitomized luxury travel.

The world of the sport fisherman was also different. No depth finders, GPS or electric trolling motors. Even if there had been, they might not have sold well. Folks of this era had personal recollections of the Great Depression and, while fishing was recognized as a pleasurable pastime, it still reflected a subsistence skill, a means to put food on the table. "Catch-and-release" just didn't fit the common wisdom. In my father's world, doing something just for pleasure was not sufficient. Yield was needed to justify the resources expended, or so it was professed. This is the world in which I became an angler.

My older sister was soon to be married. Peter, her intended, was an air force staff sergeant she met while working in Washington, D.C. During Peter's first trip to meet his future in-laws, Dad found out that this young Bostonian had never wet a line. With this revelation, he immediately decided we should introduce Peter to the honorable pastime.

After dinner that Friday, Dad and I went to the wooded vacant lot about half a block down the street with coffee can and spade in hand. This was low, swampy ground where we could dig through the rich, moist soil to collect earthworms. There were some bait shops, of course, but worms were free and an ample supply was always available in exchange for a little labor. Why spend good money on something God provided for the taking?

At sunrise the next morning, following a substantial breakfast, we climbed into our green '50 Chevrolet Deluxe which was packed with a collection of fishing tackle. Mom sent us off with a half-dozen sandwiches and a thermos full of coffee she had stashed away in the same black lunch pail that Dad carried to work every day.

We were off on our great adventure.

It was unusual back then for a fisherman to own a boat and trailer. An avid fisherman might own a "portable" outboard motor, the might of which could be measured on a scale at about ½ hp for every 20 pounds of weight. The speed with which you could move about a lake was limited not only by what you could afford, but what you could tote from the car to the dock. Fishermen like my father, who got out less than a half-dozen times a season, considered an outboard to be a luxury and usually opted to row or just sit on shore.

Almost every farmer whose land bordered a body of water had a couple of acres on the shoreline where he kept a few picnic tables and a number of flat-bottom rowboats made from wood planks. Both were usually painted the same shade of green. Renting boats to fishermen and picnickers provided a little pocket cash and often opened up relationships with town folk who might become inclined to buy eggs and produce.

Dad paid for the boat then climbed back in the car as the farmer wished us good luck.

Just off an island, Dad lowered the concrete anchor and tied the rope off on the wooden rail that supported the seats.

Pete had just purchased a brand new rod and reel.

Dad had his trusty 4-foot steel rod with its red glass eyelets that glowed in the sunlight like five rubies mounted on the length of a shining black rapier.

I was given a 10-foot bamboo pole with about 15 feet of 30-pound-test braided nylon line tied to the wire eyelet at its tip. On the line was a painted cork bobber, which was attached by passing the line through a hole in its center and held in place by a tapered wood peg inserted at the top. A couple of split shot and a hook at the end of a short piece of monofilament leader made up the balance of the rig. Dad threaded a worm on the hook and tossed it in the water with the instruction, "Keep your eye on your bobber. When it goes under, lift it up and pull the fish into the boat."

As Dad turned his attention to Peter to share some of the fine points of casting, my bobber suddenly disappeared with a resounding "Bloup" as the water crashed in on the hole where it had sat just the instant before. The pole doubled over and I had to wedge myself between the gunwales, hanging on to keep from being yanked out of the boat. The narrow little boat rocked back and forth as the water boiled from somewhere under the rod tip. In the midst of all this turmoil Dad was shouting, "Hang on! Don't lose it! Hang on!"

For my part, I was scared to death and hanging on for dear life. On one hand, whatever was on the other end of that line was about to pull me in with it. (An idea that held little appeal at the moment.) On the other hand, if I did land it, I wasn't sure I wanted to be joined in this little boat by whatever was trying so hard to have me join it in the lake. But as excited as Dad was, I knew this had to be something really great. I knew if I did manage to land whatever was at the other end of that line, I could bask in the warmth of my father's pride for days.

I hung on to that pole and struggled to keep both it and me out of the water while Dad and Peter became my cheering section.

"Hang on!"

"Keep your pole up."

"You can land it!"

"Pull! Pull!"

I wanted to pass the pole off to my father, but he insisted I continue the fight.

"You hooked it, you can land it! Get it up beside the boat and I'll get the net under it."

With the same violent suddenness with which the bobber had disappeared, the line shot back out of the water as the leader gave way and the fish and I parted company.

In a moment, the boat settled down and all became quiet except for the disappointed consolations of my elders.

"Too bad!"

"You almost had it."

"What a fight!"

"What do you figure it was?"

"Big northern, I guess. Maybe a dogfish."

"I wonder if we can hook it again?"

HOOK IT AGAIN? At that moment I had some mixed feelings about tangling with that monster a second time. To me it hadn't been at all clear just who had been trying to make lunch of whom.

We came home with our limit of sunfish later that afternoon. Out came the Kodak to record the event and we had one heck of a fish fry that night. But the talk of the evening, and for that matter the following week,

was the "fight of a lifetime" and "the one that got away" and how proud we were of how the boy hung on. "He would have landed it for sure if the line hadn't broken."

But the story here is not about the one that got away, but the one that got hooked for life. The adventure, the excitement and the praise of valor in a fight well fought, made for one really great memory.

Things are a lot different today. Gone are the farm accesses, picnic grounds, wooden boats and the cattle standing in the lake. For better or worse, our values as sportsmen have changed a lot too. We have so much more. Luxury boats, high horsepower motors and all kinds of electronic assistance. We see our sport now as pure recreation or a contest of skill for skill's sake rather than a reflection of the quest for survival.

But after 50 years, that memory still remains as sharp as if it happened this afternoon. It is the foundation on which a lifelong passion is built. Every kid needs a memory like that. One so powerful that it can transform an old man's heart into that of a little boy, every time he gets on the water.

Daniel Gendreau
Blaine, Minnesota

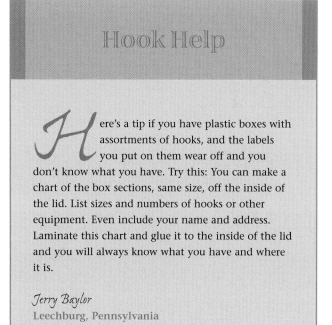

Hook Help

Here's a tip if you have plastic boxes with assortments of hooks, and the labels you put on them wear off and you don't know what you have. Try this: You can make a chart of the box sections, same size, off the inside of the lid. List sizes and numbers of hooks or other equipment. Even include your name and address. Laminate this chart and glue it to the inside of the lid and you will always know what you have and where it is.

Jerry Baylor
Leechburg, Pennsylvania

My First Time Fishing

I remember when I was about 5, my dad took me to a small pond within a 5-minute walk from my grandmother's house. We skipped stones and he told me about how his dad had taken him fishing for panfish at this very same pond when he was my age. I asked if I could try fishing there. He said that he probably had some hooks and sinkers lying around, so yes, I could.

That night after dinner, we drove out there and cut a small sapling tree down, because our rods were either broken or lost, and rigged it up with line tied to the end and a hook-and-sinker "combo." Early the next morning, I woke him up because I was too excited to sleep and told him that we had to go fishing now. He got dressed, and after we had breakfast, he said that we needed some bait. I followed him outside, where, lo and behold, he started digging in the garden right beside the carrots. I asked him what he was doing and he replied, "Getting bait." He then reached down and picked up what looked like a floppy stick. On closer examination, though, I saw it was a worm.

"We're going to use that?" I exclaimed.

"Well, yes, we are," said Dad.

We collected a small yogurt container of worms and prepared to fish. I got my boots on, and he rummaged through the drawers in the kitchen and came up with a bobber.

"What's that for?" I asked.

"So you can see when you get a bite," Dad replied.

We brought along a bucket so I could see the fish when we caught some. We walked the 5 minutes it took to get to the "hot spot," and rigged up. Being young, I didn't really want anything to do with the worms, so I let him hook them. He showed me how to put the bobber on the line and put on a worm. He tossed the line out about 5 feet or so and told me to watch the bobber, and when it went under the water, to pull the stick up. I followed his direction to the tiniest detail (which wasn't very tiny).

When that bobber went down, I pulled on that stick so hard that the small perch that had taken my worm came flying at my head. I ducked and my dad almost caught it. By almost, I mean that it fell in his lap. He said, "Hey, there ya' go, your first fish, and a nice perch, too."

He put some water in the bucket and then unhooked the fish and put it in also. After the first, there was no stopping me. We had to keep on emptying the bucket to fit more fish in. I would've fished right into the night if we hadn't run out of worms. Since then, until I was about 11, that has been my favorite thing about going to Grandma's house. Once my family heard how much fun I had, they always accompanied me on the outings. Eventually I was able to hook my own worms, and I got a better rod, but my grandmother still keeps that stick in her basement as a memento.

Over the years, I have tried leeches, dew worms and jigs, but the garden worms under a bobber on a number 10 long-shank hook with a small split shot always caught more fish. That just goes to show, even with all the new lures and gadgets being invented today, sometimes it's better to go back to the basics and remember our childhood. I still fish, and not much differently either. I see fancy crankbaits and spinner baits, but as soon as I switch to a worm, I get memories of times lost—and lots of fish!

Morgan Edwards
Toronto, Ontario, Canada

Fishing Fever

About 5 years ago, during the winter, my fishing buddy Darb called and said he wouldn't be fishing anymore. He had developed macular degeneration and was declared legally blind. Part of me fell apart! He and I had fished many lakes through the years. Each spring he'd get "fishing fever." We'd load up two or three other buddies and spend the whole day touring various lakes, having lunch together and talking about fishing.

Darb sold his boat and gave all his rods and tackle to the grandchildren. He said he could never fish again.

Another Memorial Day was coming up. Les, another fishing buddy, and I had been slaying foot-long perch in an unknown small lake. Perch were Darb's favorite target. I called Darb and told him we'd pick him up at 7:00 a.m. As strongly and loudly as he declined, I wouldn't take no for an answer.

We helped him into the boat. I baited the hook and told him to fish just over the side. He always did catch perch by feel anyway. By noon Darb had caught 15 jumbo perch.

On the way home he said, "This is the best fishing day I think I ever had. I didn't think I'd ever catch a fish again."

I'm not much for tears but my eyes did get a little wet.

Earle A. Hanselmann
Lu Verne, Iowa

Why Throw Away Those Old Topcoating Buckets?

If you have two old topcoating or other buckets, remove the lids but keep one. Measure and cut the bottom off of one bucket about 6 inches up from the bottom. Drill two holes across from each other about ½ inch from the top. Run a piece of heavy cord through the holes, bring them together at the middle, and tie the ends together. Set this aside.

Mark the other (whole) bucket at three equal spots around the side of the bucket, 6 to 6½ inches from the top; drill a ¼-inch hole at each mark. Insert a ¼-inch bolt through the hole, and add a nut on the inside; tighten. Now set the bottom with the string in the top, add the lid and you're done!

Minnow bucket fits in the bottom. Hooks, sinkers, handwarmers, whatever you want, fit in the top. Plus you have a seat to sit on. This is a great helper for fishing spillways in late fall or winter. I have even brought live fish home in the bottom of the bucket.

Ron Huff
New Phila, Ohio

Gone but Not Forgotten— a Message to a Friend

Sneaking out just before sunrise to catch an hour of undisturbed fishing before the rest of the cabin stirred to life. Watching the boys scatter to the far corners of the boat as I cradled your first muskie and they realized how big it was and how menacing its teeth looked. Watching you cast a popper into a tree, pull it loose, bounce it off a rock and then see it inhaled by a 5-pound largemouth. And, of course, just sitting on the porch watching another beautiful sunset over Stony Lake. Memories to last a lifetime. Memories to help remember a friend who left this world far too soon.

Dave Warriner died this year at the age of 42, leaving behind a wonderful wife, Jan, and three great sons, David Jr., Nick and John. He also left behind fond memories for all who knew him, and for that we are eternally grateful. We met 5 years ago at a cold ice skating rink, as our sons became members of the same youth hockey team. They bonded immediately, as did our families. I remember the first time I told Dave about my annual trips to Stony Lake in Southeastern Ontario and seeing his eyes light up. It didn't take much arm twisting to convince him to join me that summer and each summer thereafter. I also remember the look of excitement and wonder as we pulled into the camp and he and his family got their first look at Stony Lake. Dave and his boys had their lines in the water before the car was half unloaded (leaving me with the pleasant chore of finishing that task).

That first year it was obvious that a freshwater fisherman he was not. Fishing for back bay flounder, sea bass on the wrecks or snapper blues just outside the surf was more his forte. Actually, that character flaw of his helped me to become a better fisherman. You see, my talk of 50 to 100 fish days had raised the level of expectation to the point that I had to produce. Not only did I have to produce numbers of fish, but numbers of specific species of fish. As I now think back on my memories of Dave and try to put them within the context of fishing tips, it is the little things that I remember most.

One such instance is a time we were both throwing identical Shad Raps to a rocky point. I was hitting a smallmouth on every third cast and he couldn't buy a

strike. No words were spoken, but with each fish I hooked I felt a set of eyes glaring at me. I glanced over and noticed that Dave had secured his lure using a Palomar knot. After I suggested he retie using a Rapala knot, Dave began to catch his share of fish. Little things can sometimes make a big difference.

I always loved when Dave and the boys would say to me, "Let's go out for walleye." Of course, every time those words were spoken I would be looking at a bluebird sky and a flat calm lake (where is the wind when you need it). Fishing my favorite 12- to 14-foot contours just outside the weedlines had not a chance of working under those conditions. So off we would go to Burleigh Falls to try our luck in the current, or to the rock Dave and his boys fed to those fish. Or the dirty looks my son, Michael, would get as he pulled up another walleye. It took awhile (and a lot of bait) to understand the importance of keeping your jig as vertical as possible and setting the hook at the slightest indication of a strike.

I love smallmouth fishing. I know where they are and I know how to catch them. However, Dave and his sons' quest to catch as many different species as possible also helped me realize the pleasures of going after old bucket mouth. We learned together how to go deep into the weed flats and identify the potentially productive open pockets. We also found out together that light tackle just doesn't cut it in these conditions. Jig fishing in heavy cover on anything less than 15-pound test just damages the resource because break-offs are almost a certainty.

My one regret is not landing young David's first muskie. Throwing bucktails in a shallow, weedy, rocky bay with the wind kicking up a storm, David hooked into a nice 40-plus-inch fish. The next few minutes looked more like a Keystone Cops movie than anything else. With Dave and David fishing off the stern, me at the bow working the trolling motor, and my son, Michael, next to me, we were all caught off guard when the fish hit. As the muskie broke water the first time, Michael took off to get the cradle, which of course (unknown to us at the time) was stowed neatly away in another boat. Dave, who was as afraid of a muskie's teeth as his son, headed for the bow as I headed for the stern to help David. This resulted in our crashing into one another at the walk-through windshield. Through all of this David just held on, fighting the fish as best he could. By the time those of us who were supposed to know what we were doing got our act together, the muskie took one final leap, spit the lure and retreated back into the weeds without having to endure the trauma of having its picture taken. As we watched the fish swim away and the disappointment on young David's face, a valuable lesson was learned—have the necessary equipment readily at hand and make sure all in the boat

know their responsibilities, either in helping or in getting out of the way.

I will miss you, my friend, and I thank you for the memories you gave me. Rest assured, your boys will be at my side this summer feeding leeches to the walleye, hunting the elusive muskie and fondly remembering a great person, friend and father.

Thanks, Dave. You will be missed.

Albert Herhal
Pottstown, Pennsylvania

Snappy Lure Changes

*T*his tip makes sense when you use a snap to change lures. Use it on a spinnerbait to keep it in place. Cut a ⅛-inch piece of surgical tubing and place it on the nose of the spinnerbait to keep the snap in place.

Charles Been
Butler, Pennsylvania

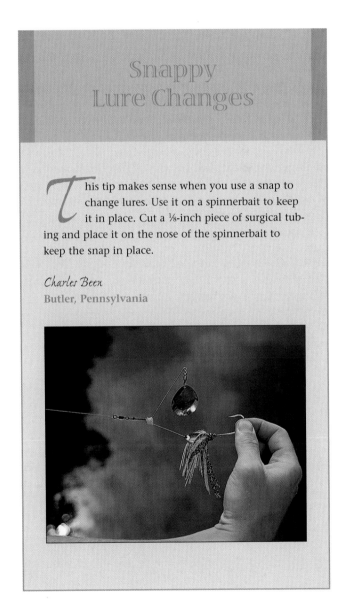

Fly-Fishing Follies

While fly fishing with a number 18 black gnat at a pond near our house, I was hoping to catch some crappie, but instead caught a much wider variety of species.

My first cast landed perfectly on a weed 20 feet behind me. Using all the grace that comes with being a fly fisherman, I grunted and tried to pull on the line to get the fly unsnagged. All of my tugging was causing the grass to rustle quite a bit, and to my horror I discovered that dozens of bullfrogs were leaving the water to attack my fly.

I gasped and charged the fly, trying to scare the frogs away. I grabbed my line, and after a brief struggle managed to land an angry bullfrog. I carefully released him and went back to my fishing.

After several more casts, a large dragonfly grabbed my small fly in mid-cast and tried to fly off with it, but he didn't put up near the fight that the frog did.

I managed to catch several small crappie, but my largest catch was yet to come.

By some stroke of luck, I got my fly to land on the water. I felt a strike and set the small hook into the mouth of a 3½-inch tadpole.

The fight was very brief, but the memories of that strange day will last forever.

Jesse Williams
Davenport, Nebraska

Protect Your Boat

Do you have problems with rodents getting under your boat cover, and chewing up wiring? I did. Each year I would have to rewire most of my boat. Now whenever I put on my cover, I throw a handful of mothballs in the boat. They also seem to keep out cats.

Victor Leake
Mannford, Oklahoma

My Tale

When we think of going fishing we think about catching those great big bucket mouths or mooneyes, but that is not always the case. You may not believe this, but not everyone goes out there just for the "rush," but also to get in touch with those who made them the person they are today.

You may not know where I, a 15-year-old boy, am coming from with all these words, but I lost my father a few years ago. He was great. And he was quite the fisherman, also being involved with Ottawa BASS Pro Tournament Fishing. He would always place in the top five, and won many tournaments.

He taught my older sister, younger brother, mother and me all how to be successful fishermen.

He taught us how to fish on Clayton Lake, just outside of Almonte, Ontario. Clayton Lake has a number of species of fish including pickerel, northern pike, mudpout, sucker, large- and smallmouth bass, and numerous types of panfish.

I have to say that I fish at least 3 days a week during the summer, and there's not one moment while I am out on that lake I do not think about my father. Sometimes when I am out on the lake by myself I just gaze off into the sky and ask, "Why, why did you have to leave us, father, at such a young age?"

I know he is happy where he is now, and every time I catch a fish I feel my dad is watching over me and made that fish bite my line.

This is why I feel that fishing on the lake on that hot humid day isn't all about getting that great big "rush" when that 6-pound bucket mouth jumps out of the water at your Frog Wild fishing lure. Fishing's also about getting in touch with yourself, and the ones who made you who you are.

Jesse John Lowe
Clayton, Ontario, Canada

Mark Your Lures

I mark on the bellies of my crankbaits with a permanent marker if it is either a floating, sinking, or suspending crankbait.

Charles M. Simon
Hoffman Estates, Illinois

Spooling Remedy

When loading your reels with fresh line, place the filler spool in a pail of water. The spool will float and turn easily as line is wound onto your reel. The water adds enough friction to prevent overruns and backlashes. Plus, the water softens the line and reduces memory.

Erick Farrington
Ewing, New Jersey

A Lesson Learned

As the parent, I'm supposed to be the one to teach the child, but a few year ago my daughter taught me a valuable lesson.

It was a time when I was trying to get into bass fishing and not doing so well. The harder I tried the less fun I had, and fewer pay checks came my way.

On this particular day my young daughter and I were spending the day fishing. I had a tournament coming up in a week and wanted to find some bass.

I fixed up a light spin-casting rod and reel for her with a hair jig and a bobber so that she could fish from the back of the boat while I searched for largemouth bass from the front. Her giggling and laughter floated over the water and acted like sandpaper on my nerves as I worked myself into a frenzy. No matter how many fish I caught, they never came fast enough nor were they ever large enough to please me.

From time to time she would call my attention to a bird or butterfly on the bank. She was always amazed at nature, but I was too busy to notice.

Soon the muscles in my neck tightened up and the pain was becoming unbearable. I had been wounded in the army some years before and the bullets tore up the muscles in my back. Each time I tried to fish all day the pain would become too great, and the VA was talking about more surgery.

As the pain grew, I sat down in the boat, upset that I could not even make it through a day of fishing. Sitting in the bottom of my boat I watched as my daughter enjoyed even the smallest sunfish that would bite her lure. While taking a small perch off the line for her, I pointed out the markings on the fish, and I realized that I was beginning to relax. Soon I was pointing out squirrels on the bank and once even a deer. The pain left my back as I thanked each fish that bit, showing how pretty they were to Kerri.

After that day my fishing improved as did my outlook on life. My daughter taught me to put the fun back into fishing. More relaxed now, I find myself at the pay window a lot more often, and even when I don't get a check I still have fun, and I always take the time to enjoy the day.

Now I'm a grandfather and I can't wait to see what my grandchildren will teach me. One other thing; I never did have to have that surgery.

Victor Leake
Mannford, Oklahoma

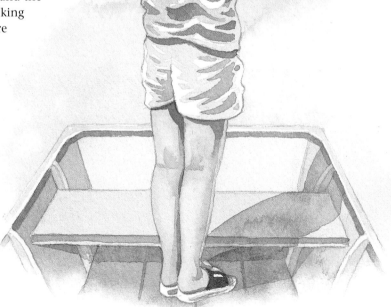

Splashy Casts

When fly fishing for panfish in slightly murky water, don't worry if your cast makes a slight splash on the water when it lands. Often this small splash will attract fish.

Jesse Williams
Davenport, Nebraska

Tubebait Tip

The use of tubebaits is growing, but they are light and hard to throw without extra weight. So slide a salt craw inside the hollow part of the tube; now it has more weight for flipping and more "body" that the large fish love.

Victor Leake
Mannford, Oklahoma

Fishing Tips for Kids

Hey, kids, the next time you hear your parents whine that they are bored and have nothing to do, take them fishing! Tell them it's not a contest of having the best fishing tackle or about catching the largest trophy fish, it's about spending quality time together.

Relaxing in the great outdoors doesn't get any better than a family fishing trip, so keep reminding your parents of how much fun fishing is. If it is a really hot day, I suggest river fishing because there are many shady spots for Mom and Dad to retreat to. Moms and Dads often get a little cranky when it's hot, so be patient with them, especially when their line is all tangled up. Kids, you may have to help your parents up and down the banks with the equipment, so be prepared.

I prefer nightcrawlers and minnows when I fish a river (because they're easy and they work), but occasionally I get creative with lures. Usually when I fish with lures along a river I catch most everything but fish. So kids, don't be embarrassed or ashamed of Mom or Dad when you see their hook or lure hung up in a tree. It's perfectly normal for this to happen occasionally.

Kids, when you catch a fish bigger than Mom's or Dad's, it is a good idea to let them hold your fish while you take a picture of them. Remember kids, sometimes it takes patience to catch a fish, but it takes even more patience when you're trying to teach your parents how to fish! It is very important to remind your parents not to litter because leaving trash behind is very bad for the environment. You may have to pick up after your parents when you are getting ready to leave the fishing spot.

Last, but not least, make sure your parents keep their membership current with North American Fishing Club. Truly, the most important fishing tip of all. Happy fishing!

Kevin Sandell
Guilford, New York

Left Oar! Right Oar!

When I was a kid one of the hardest things I had to learn was how to row the boat for Dad.

I always felt like I was with Washington crossing the Delaware and when the General said, "Quiet, men!" my oar would splash and squeak, alerting all the Hessians. The finesse of rowing a boat escaped me.

Of course, Dad was very experienced at that sort of thing. Ever since Bagnell Dam filled the Lake of the Ozarks in 1931, he'd fished all over the lake, from The Grand Glaze to Warsaw. And he did it all in rented wooden rowboats, sometimes with a 5-hp motor. When I was a kid all of Dad's various fishing spots looked alike to me, even though some were 60 miles apart. The lake was pretty deep, from 60 to 100 feet in the wide reaches. Because of its hundreds of tributaries and the deep, sunken current of the old Osage River, the Lake of the Ozarks was never clean. The water was gunmetal gray and always with a slight chop. The shores were wooded or lined with steep, ancient limestone bluffs. There were thousands of coves and inlets. Dad tried to fish them all. Remarkably, he never owned his own boat.

Because of his great experience, he knew how to row with the expertise of a Viking. He could bring a sluggish 14-foot wooden boat alongside a bushy or rocky band and cast ahead to where the roots of a sunken tree or the tops of big rocks poked above the water. If he got his lure to just the right spot, in between two roots or at the base of a rock, he would often get a strike.

But whether Dad got a strike or not, it was the perfect cast that mattered to him. He took more satisfaction in getting his lure to the right place than in catching the fish that was supposed to be there.

It was his father, the Reverend John L., who taught him those values. My grandpa was the first to earn a living with his wits instead of working the land. He was always on the cutting edge of technology. He fished using artificial lures and hand-tied flies. As a kid, Dad was happy to fish with a cane pole or a trotline. But when he saw his dad catching big fish using bass plugs and a casting rod he changed his mind. Grandpa taught Dad how to cast from a boat and how to maneuver the boat to just the right spot for a perfect cast.

So Dad was a master at controlling a rowboat and making the perfect cast.

When Dad was trying to teach me to fish, he did all the rowing for me. When I came along he naturally thought that I would learn the same skills. He was enthralled by the idea of raising a clone of himself.

Little did he know what the reality would be. I admired his skill, and the first thing I learned to do was to make the perfect cast. Sometimes I caught fish, but most of the time I didn't.

All of that was well and good as long as my "guide" was rowing for me. But pretty soon, I realized that Dad wanted to fish too. As soon as I learned to cast well, Dad told me to change ends with him so that I could row and he could fish. So the neophyte took over.

I sat in the control center. I hefted the oars. They swung easily in their locks. I looked behind me. That was where we were supposed to go.

"OK, kid, remember when you pull the right oar, the boat goes left. The left oar brings the boat right. Got it?" This was practically the extent of his teaching. "Both oars is full speed ahead. Push on the oars for a full stop. Push on one oar and pull on the other for a speed turn. Got that?"

"Uh …" I said, uncertainly.

"OK, let's go!" I manned the oars, dipped them in the water and pulled. A mighty splash from the left oar sent the bow right. I had not intended that. I pulled the right oar to bring us back on course, and pulled deep with both oars.

"I want to fish that point," Dad said, pointing over my shoulder, "Then into the cove and back around all the brush in the shallow end, then back up the other side. Let's go, both oars!"

Rowing is hard work. It's not so bad when going flat out in deep water, but I discovered that I was expected to navigate like Nelson at Trafalgar.

"OK, even her out and let me get a crack at that stump," Dad would say. That meant stop oars and push a little with the left. "Come on, get closer," Dad urged. I would pull mightily with both oars.

"Hold it!" Dad said softly. Stop oars. Here came the cast from the World Master. It was too far out. I could see Dad's pained look. So I pulled with both oars to get closer. "Wait a minute," Dad cried, "I'm trying to reel in!" Dad reeled frantically, making the topwater lure do things that no fish would believe.

"Let her go, now, we're coming in." I leaned on the oars. A slight current or something made the oars two tillers and the boat skewed to the left.

"Right oar!" Dad ordered. Right oar it was. The boat lost way and turned right, but did not straighten out. "Left oar, for cryin' out loud!" Dad fumed. Dad had not explained to me about compensation. It was always just, "Left oar!", then, "Right oar!" He probably thought that

I would instinctively know how to compensate. But this detail must have been left out of my DNA. I had to learn by sad experience and of that I had plenty.

Although my rowing was at best only satisfactory, Dad did try to do a lot of fishing while I was at the oars. The situations would have been hilarious to anyone else, but for us it was torture. Dad could never quite reach the log, the rock or the pool that he wanted. Or we would be too close and he would catch a tree. However, Dad would never directly criticize me for putting the boat in the wrong place. He treated my mistakes like some circumstance over which he had no control.

But he would always vocalize: "Left oar! Right oar!"

As I have said, when Dad was rowing he always put the boat just where it should be. I studied his style, but I couldn't figure out how he did it.

I continued to botch things up. But the worst times were when Dad would actually catch a fish and had to rely on me to keep the boat straight so he could land it. "Bring her around," he would plead. "Get the oar out of the way! You've got my line! Oh, great, he got off!"

Then there was gloom and tension. My face was grim and my throat tight and I fought tears. There was nothing worse than Dad losing a fish because I had done something wrong. The only thing that might have been worse was once, when I was backcasting, my lure whizzed through the air in a low trajectory and hit Dad right in the head!

"OK, kid," Dad would say with remarkable patience, "Let's get in there and try again." This particular time I was successful in wrenching our craft to the right spot and Dad actually caught another fish. This time he didn't say a word. With tongue between his teeth and a gleam in his eye, he landed a 3-pound bass. It hung, dripping and flipping over the boat.

Then Dad smiled and said, "Not bad, kid," as if he didn't really mind all my goofs.

But then, his face changed. "Back oars! We're going ashore!"

Oh, Lord, the overhanging branches were hitting the boat. I ducked, but Dad couldn't. The tree limbs just missed his head and scraped his body. With his hands in front of his face, he growled, "Get us out of here. The fishing is ruined now, anyway."

There are many tales about how I learned to row a boat. But the fact is, I could never row to suit my dad. And though he was pained, injured and frustrated, he never ridiculed me or brought it up with anyone else. When it came to rowing for myself later in life, everything Dad said miraculously came back to me. Today, I can put a rowboat just about anywhere. And though Dad is gone, I can still hear in my mind his big voice saying, "Left oar! Right oar! Come on, kid, let's go!"

Dave McKinsey
Novato, California

Opening Day

Many years ago, in my home state of Massachusetts, there was a fishing phenomenon known as Opening Day. Generally Opening Day was the third Saturday in April, which meant that somewhere around February first, I started getting my gear together. After all, it never hurt to be ready, just in case the state decided to pull a fast one and open the season ahead of time.

One memorable season I packed my gear in the car the night before and waited for the right time to leave for my favorite spot. Sleep was usually out of the question for me. If I did nod off, I would be constantly looking at the clock all night, to make sure I didn't oversleep. I got to my friend Bubba's house, right on schedule, and as usual he was sound asleep. I pounded on the door for 20 minutes, honked the horn and woke up half his neighborhood.

After several threats from Bubba's neighbors, I climbed through an open window and woke him up. "Come on, let's get going," I shouted. "What's your hurry?" Bubba replied. "We're going to miss out on the best spot." I answered. "Besides, it'll be light soon." "It's only 2 in the morning," Bubba snapped. (Bubba was always nasty when he first woke up.) "Quit whining and get dressed," I said.

Thirty minutes later, we were on our way. There was an air of silence in the car because we weren't talking to each other. I was steamed about Bubba's indifference to the importance of Opening Day. He just didn't understand the importance of getting there first. My favorite spot was about 20 miles away. We got there in about 12 minutes. I had to put the pedal to the metal to make up for Bubba's tardiness.

When we got to the stream, I had to pry Bubba's fingers from my dashboard. "Nice going, now it will take months to get those 10 finger marks out of there." Bubba was still trying to rub some circulation back into his fingers while I hopped into my waders.

I put on my vest, grabbed the net, bait and fishing rod, and headed for my spot. "The brook is right over heeeaugh …" I took one more step and plunged 30 feet down into some brush and trees. My waders were cut and my rod was snapped in two pieces. As I lay there, cut and bleeding, I heard someone say, "What was that?" "Don't worry. It's only my brother," another voice responded. "Great." My brother Dave had beaten me to the fishing hole.

I was really angry with Bubba now. This was all his fault. Had he gotten up on time, Dave would have never gotten there first. I swapped my torn waders and broken rod with Bubba, who was sleeping in the back seat. I limped back down to the stream (this time with flashlight in hand) and proceeded to wait for daylight. Three hours later, it was light enough to fish. Numbness had begun to set in, and I was having a hard time casting. "I'll never forgive Bubba for this," I said. "I'm so numb, I can't even fish." "It could have something to do with the 37°F water," Dave replied.

After another hour or so, I couldn't take it anymore. I was tired, cold and hungry, not to mention extremely sore. Reluctantly, I decided to call it quits. I limped out of the brook and headed home.

Later that afternoon, my neighbor and long-time fishing arch rival stopped over to gloat. Lucky Louie, as he was called by some, came over to show me the nice stringer of fat brook trout he had caught that afternoon. (Lucky Louie is not what I called him.) "Got to wait till the sun warms the water a bit, this time of year," Louie babbled. "They were biting like crazy at the old fishing hole you showed me last year. Funny thing was, someone cleared a nice place for me to fish in the trees and brush," he said. "Good thing, too, I forgot my waders at home."

That was about all I cared to hear. I threw Louis out of the house and went back inside to change my bandages. "Louie is like Bubba," I growled. "He'll never understand the true meaning of Opening Day," I muttered to myself. "Guys like them just never seem to catch on …" "By the way," I thought, "I wonder how Bubba got home?"

Raymond E. Lemieux Jr.
Wolcott, New York

Finesse Fishing

I was hanging around my favorite tackle shop the other day replacing the last 20 or 30 stickbaits I'd sacrificed to the fish gods, when an obvious novice to the sport of fishing plunked a 9-inch plug on the counter. I had a flashback to my younger days, fishing with my friends, the Fillpot twins, (Newton the Mutant and Freddie the Frog) and Bubba Basco.

We were fishing in our secret spot, down behind the old slaughterhouse. Fish seemed to grow extremely large there; however, we were never allowed to eat any of them. I was using the state-of-the-art tubular steel telescopic rod, 50-pound-test Japanese silk line, and a new level-wind casting reel, which I never really could cast with.

To compensate for the reel's lack of performance, I was known to cast a 9-inch Bass-O-Reno plug with four 2/0 sets of treble hooks on it. On my second cast of the day (after clearing the bird's nest from my first), I reared back and gave a hefty toss. "Stuck," I thought, and without looking, gave the line two or three tugs to clear the obstruction. All of a sudden, there was an ungodly scream and Newton took off down the shoreline like a rocket. His arms were waving madly in all directions, and he was shrieking at the top of his lungs. My line was whipping off the reel and my reel was starting to smoke (drag systems not being all that great in those days).

Fortunately, Bubba had the presence of mind to tackle Newton just as I was about to be spooled. "Sit on his chest while I look for my trusty, rusty pliers," I yelled. My pliers were a junky old pair of vise grips, not equipped with wire cutters.

One set of hooks had pierced Newton's lower lip, with the barb clear out the other side. While Bubba held him down, I locked onto the treble hooks and gave a mighty pull. The hook came out neat, but not clean. It had a vee-shaped wedge of lip skin on the end of the barb. Freddie walked Newton home, while Bubba and I returned to our fishing. Newton talked kind of funny after that. He had trouble pronouncing certain vowels, thus the nickname, "Newton the Mutant." Kids were cruel in those days.

Raymond E. Lemieux Jr.
Wolcott, New York

Easy, Organized Tackle

Many anglers find it convenient to carry their tackle in a plastic 5-gallon bucket. A strip of Styrofoam glued to the inside, near and parallel to the top, is a convenient and safe place to hang lures and snelled hooks.

John R. Campbell
Cascade, Maryland

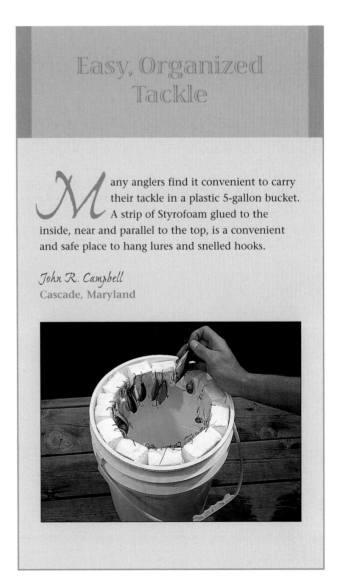

The Day I Went Fishing

The reason I got interested in fishing is because of my 5-year-old son, Cody. We went to our local store and bought our first fishing gear and license.

We went fishing for the first time and discovered it was lots of fun. I had a blast with my family. That's when I decided we were going fishing from then on. We make a trip to the river or lake every weekend.

I'm glad I found something my family can enjoy together. My other two sons, Shane, 4, and Duncan, 3, enjoy our fishing trips. They all have their own fishing rods, and they cast like pros, trying to catch a fish. Shane is a natural-born fisherman. One time he cast out with no bait, just a hook, and caught a fish.

The other day my son asks me, when are we going to buy a boat, and I told him, maybe soon. He asked again, why haven't we? My answer to him was, maybe one of these days we will have a boat.

Cody has always wanted to go fishing and camping since he was only a year old. This kid likes the outdoors and, because of my son, I'm beginning to like it very much!

Juan M. Tovar
San Angelo, Texas

Inexpensive Boat Accessories

An old friend told me that *boat* means, "a hole in the water you throw money into." So if I can save a few dollars here and there, I'll have more money to throw into my little hole in the water. When I bought my boat last year (this is my first boat), it had an extension cord reel on the front, and I really liked it. So I thought that I would put one in the back 'cause my anchor line kept getting tangled up. When I found out that they cost around $45 I changed my mind and went to the hardware store and bought an extension cord reel for about $5. I still had money left over to throw into my hole in the water.

If you think about it, this tip could help you catch more fish, too. Take the money you save and go out and buy more lures!

William Fortner
St. Paul, Indiana

A Fisherman's Lucky Day

The osprey's dive was awesome, as he touched down on the lake.
It seemed that all the fish that day were just for him to take.
A fish clenched in his talons, he flew off to his nest,
Passed the offering to his mate—then off—no time to rest.
Next, the ducklings, following in their mother's shimmering wake,
The handsome, brilliant colors of the unassuming drake.
A lean and gaunt coyote came padding down the beach,
Occasionally jumping in to seek a fish just out of reach.
Opening up my ice chest, I was more than surprised to see,
What a fine, delicious lunch my wife had packed for me.
The day passed very slowly, as I languished in the sun,
The fish were just not biting, but I was having lots of fun.
Later came the sunset, in all its brilliant glory,
So I headed back to camp without a big fish story,
So there I was in camp, a camper on a truck,
I hadn't caught a fish that day, but I'd had a lot of luck.
I just sat there in silence, there was nothing I could say,
How can I tell the others I've had "A fisherman's lucky day"?

—Paul H. Wells
San Carlos Lake, Arizona

Tangle Free

Lure covers are good for safety and they prevent tangles with other rods. Make lure covers from cheap pieces of vinyl and Velcro. Cut the vinyl into squares or rectangles; place Velcro A material on the inside of one edge, put Velcro B on opposite end, fold in the center and lace around rod, line and lure. Make the covers tight enough to stay in place even when standing in rod-storage holders. These will both provide safety and eliminate tangles with other lures and lines.

Paul H. Wells
San Carlos Lake, Arizona

Label Line When Respooling

Every time I respool a reel I take an extra 30 seconds to label it. I note the weight and date, using a self-stick label on the inside as well as the outside of the spool. "6 8/02" lets me know it is 6-pound test, respooled August 2002. Pencil works best and lasts longest for marking the label.

Dr. Robert L. Josephs
Palm Bay, Florida

The Getaway

My story begins last summer on a nice day in late July. It was a beautiful day and I decided to ask my Dad to drop me at the lake for a few hours.

On the way, we picked up a few friends. One was Nathan Hille. He is a buddy of mine who doesn't do much fishing, so when he comes with me, the first half hour is always a reminder period or a learning period. The second friend is Jesse Sturm. He actually lives on the lake so I call him before I come so he has a chance to get his boat ready. After we picked up Nathan, our next stop was the bait shop to get some garden worms and some nightcrawlers.

Oh, it seems I have forgotten to tell you what I fish. I usually fish bluegills, perch and largemouth bass. Well, the next stop just happened to be the lake, so we landed my 14-foot Mirrocraft with an 8-hp Mercury outboard engine on the back and a trolling motor on the front. Nathan and I took off for Jesse's house. We met him in front of his house. Then, in the two boats, we headed off to a little hot spot I have for some early morning bluegills.

Well, the day went by and we caught a few here and there, just enough for a good meal. Well, noon rolled around and it got really hot, like 80 to 85°F and since the bluegills had died off for a while and the water was pretty decent temperature, we decided to head to a little sand spot off a point on the lake. It is really sandy from the shore to about 100 yards out where there is a steep drop from 1 foot to 8 feet with good weed structure.

My buddies were out messing around swimming and racing each other in the water while I saw it as a perfect opportunity to pick up some more bluegills. The first cast my bobber went down and I picked up a little bluegill.

The next cast I had another one on, or so I thought. It seemed to be a bluegill with some decent weight. Then, I saw it swim by. It was a huge perch, at least 14 inches long, which is very big for Shawano Lake. Since I had waded away from my boat to the drop, all I had was my rod, which had 4-pound test on it for bluegills. I got very excited and tried to lift him into my hand; then the line twisted, he spun and his spiny dorsal hit my hand. It hurt, so I jerked my hand back and lifted his head out of the water and he jumped and snapped the line. He got away.

Cody Krueger
Shawano, Wisconsin

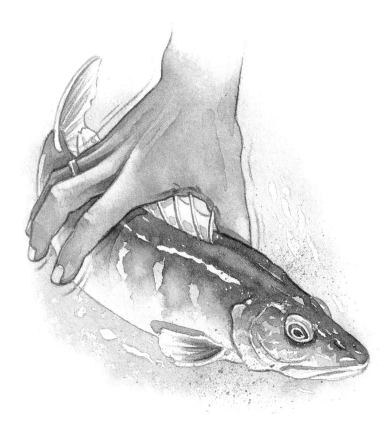

Playing Around

My tip is that if you ever get a big one on, always play them until they're tired and then put them in the net and in the boat.

Cody Krueger
Shawano, Wisconsin

Glad I Wasn't Alone!

I was fishing in the Big Walnut Creek with a few friends of mine. We were fishing for rock bass. It was just before dark; you know, when it is really hard to see if you only have a flashlight. We were just about ready to pack things up and head home. I looked at my pole and had a small bite, so I jerked it and started reeling it in. At first I thought I had a turtle because it wasn't putting up a fight. Then I saw that it was a carp. I kept reeling it in. Remember, it was dark out. When I got it to the bank, I pulled it into the weeds. All of a sudden there was a terrible smell. It was very nasty, to say the least. It was the carp. It was dead. I could not believe it. I knew I had had a bite, but how? The carp was dead. So I pulled on my line so that I could look in its mouth. I was amazed at what I found. There was a crawdad inside of the carp. He must have pulled my bait into the carp's mouth. No one could believe it. Including me. That's why I named this story, "Glad I Wasn't Alone!" Here's my tip:

• It is safer to fish with someone than by yourself. Plus, if something like this happens to you, you'll want someone there to see it or they may not believe it.

John Wall
Reynoldsburg, Ohio

Make Some Noise

I'm a very serious ice angler and I try to be as quiet as possible when pursuing my quarry. But sometimes you have to make a little noise. My tip is very simple. It allows the angler to add a little noise or remove it. It is sometimes difficult to rattle with micro jigs, but not anymore. Here's the solution.

I buy ³⁄₁₆-inch-diameter rubber tubing. It comes in different sizes and colors. I cut it in ¾-inch pieces. I take a piece and thread it on my line, followed by a small bead and then a small swivel, to which I attach an 18-inch leader, and then my jig. The bead keeps the tubing from sliding down over the swivel when you don't want to use a rattle.

I use the mag worm rattles, but most worm rattles will work. I slide a rattle into the tube when I want to make noise or easily remove the rattle for a quiet presentation.

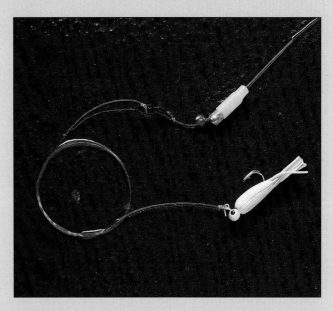

This plan works in many fishing applications and it will help you catch a few more fish. You can also pack some cotton in the tubing with a toothpick and soak it with your favorite scent for a great attractor. Good luck!

Chris Meadows
Anchorage, Alaska

Carp Power

I live in Niagara Falls, New York, so there is no shortage of places to fish and species to fish for. I enjoy fishing the lower Niagara River for salmon and steelhead and the upper river for bass and pike. I also have two sons who love to fish—Brian, who is 9 and Cameron, who is 2.

Cam is too young to bring on river trips so I take the boys to a public lake in the falls called Hyde Park. It's a great place for kids: lots of sunfish, small bass, catfish and a lot of good-sized carp. The usual routine is to set the kids up with worms and while they are catching one panfish after another I set up my salmon rod with bread balls and try to hook onto the carp, then let the kids fight the bigger fish. I always leave my bail open so I don't lose my pole because I spend the majority of the time helping out the little guys.

One day we had just gotten set up and I had just cast out my bread ball when Brian got a tangle in his line. I set the pole down and took about three steps toward him when I remembered that I had not opened the bail. Just as the thought registered, I heard the sucking sound of carp eating the bread we had thrown in. I turned around just in time to see my line go tight and my pole go flying into the water.

Not wanting to lose my good rod and reel, I took three running steps and made a headfirst dive after my gear. Not only did I get hold of the pole I also managed to land the 30-inch carp that had tried to take it. When my kids, my wife and everyone else in the area finished laughing hysterically at me, the boys wanted a picture of the fish, which was not possible because the camera was in the pack that was still attached to my waist. So there is my tale.

• My tips would be always remember to open your bail and always make sure your camera is in your tackle box!

David M. DiRienzo
Niagara Falls, New York

Before the Lake Was Here

The early fog surrounds you, as you push off from the bank,
You've decided where you're going and you give the starter rope a yank.
The engine coughs and sputters, and finally springs to life,
You're moving faster now, the wind cuts you like a knife.
You round the "Old Farm Point," your heart is filled with joy,
And your mind drifts back in time, to when you were a boy.
Then you realize you're passing over the orchard, where you stole apples every year,
And over there beyond that cove, you shot your very first deer.
Right about here, you think, was the Johnson's chicken coop,
Now you're over Hatcher's driveway whose snow you were paid to scoop.
Then, your depth finder shows, you're crossing the old river;
Is it the morning chill or the memories that make you shiver?
The sun is shining now, the magic spell is broken,
You've already had a special day, without a word being spoken.
You go about your fishing, each landing brings a cheer,
But you still remember the good times you had, before the lake was here.

—Paul H. Wells
San Carlos Lake, Arizona

Duct Tape Solution

*H*ere's an easy tip you can use both on and off the water. Every sportsman knows the benefits of duct tape, but we can't just carry a roll around everywhere we go, right? Here's what you do: Unroll about 3 feet of duct tape and lay it sticky-side-up on a table; next, place a business card on one end, and wrap the tape around it the long way, by flipping the card over and over, being careful to keep the edges lined up. Next, just fold over the last ½-inch to form a tab and keep the whole thing in your wallet, and it'll be there when you need it. Here's to tight lines and good fishing.

Jon Rasmussen
Menasha, Wisconsin

Easy Rod Eye Repair

*E*mergency rod eyes can be made from a safety pin. Cut off the head of the pin and bend the eye end up to form the emergency rod eye. Align the pin with the rod, then wrap with thread. Tie tightly and cover with clear nail polish. Replace before your next fishing trip.

Carry several sizes of pins in your toolbox or first aid kit. The thread and nail polish will take up very little room in a small repair kit.

Paul H. Wells
San Carlos Lake, Arizona

Karen's Catch

We have a cabin about 15 minutes by boat from the Illinois River at a place called Patterson Bay, just south of Bath, Illinois. We spend almost every weekend there relaxing and fishing. We do some bass and crappie fishing, but mainly tight-line fishing from the boat. We catch a variety of fish, including channel cat, carp, white perch, white bass and an occasional eel. Eels are especially fun because you get to watch some of the people go into a panic thinking they have caught a snake!

I have fished since I was old enough to hold a pole, but my wife Karen is still a novice. She is eager to learn though, so I try to teach her what I have learned through the years.

Well, a couple years ago, a few guys organized a carp tournament at Patterson Bay. The entries the second year grew even bigger than the first, so the second year the total number of fish was limited to the 12 largest, plus the smallest, largest and ugliest. There are three people allowed per boat and all entry fees are paid to the top four teams with the highest total poundage, plus the smallest, largest and ugliest fish.

Now, I have always preached to Karen about keeping her eyes on her rods at all times, since they have a tendency to disappear out of the boat very quickly at times. This has happened to me twice!

About an hour before the tournament's cutoff time, Karen reached over to get a cold one out of the cooler, turning her head for just a second. Lo and behold, her brand-new fishing pole went flying out of the boat. At first she didn't know what to say or do, as she sat there trying to decide whether to get mad or cry. Of course, I had to take the opportunity to get in a couple of "I told you so's."

Our friend Amy (the third member of our team), and I tried casting for the pole, but to no avail. With cutoff time approaching, we decided to concentrate on fishing and worry about replacing the pole later. Shortly afterward, Amy got a good bite, set the hook, and started reeling one in. As her line got closer to the boat, her hook appeared with nothing but blue Stren line coming up with it. I grabbed the line off of Amy's hook and as I started pulling the line in, guess what happened? Up came my wife's pole! As I was winding in the slack, I felt some resistance, so I turned to Karen and said, "Here, you can reel your fish in now." After I handed her the pole, she proceeded to bring in the 3-pound carp that had tried to steal it.

We all laughed as we headed back for the weigh-in, and talked about the odds of recovering her pole, with the fish still on it, in the middle of the river. We didn't finish in the top four, but I did get the smallest fish—1 pound, 11¾ inches long.

And, we had the best fish story. But we didn't win any money for that!

Butch and Karen Miller
Sherman, Illinois

Remove Line Twists

Line that has been on the spool for a long time takes a set. It curls, twists and comes off of the spool in clumps (bird's nests) when cast. To remove the set, attach a swivel and small lure. Let the line out and trail it behind the boat, letting it remain submerged for several minutes. A fast retrieve puts stress on the line and pulls out the curl.

Dr. Robert L. Josephs
Palm Bay, Florida

Pole Positions

Have you ever been out on the lake with your best fishing buddy watching him catch fish after fish? You do everything you can think of. Use the same lure. Even cast to his spot before he does. But to no avail. Maybe the only thing you're doing "wrong" is how you "hold" or "work" the pole.

Here are some "pole positions" to think about and even practice. They may help you control your lure better and even catch more fish.

1. STROKING OR JIGGING OR POPPING

Moving the pole from straight out in front of you to any position up from that, until it is straight up and down in front of you and then back down again. How far you move the pole between these 2 positions determines the length of motion to your lure. Every lure has a different action. A jig or sinking lure will move up with the up stroke and down with the down stroke or pause. Floating-diving lures dive with the up stroke and rise with the down stroke or pause. Topwater, just more forward slightly.

2. SWEEPING OR WALK THE DOG

This works the best with topwater plugs like Zara Spooks or Sluggos. After casting, take up the slack, then sweep the rod to the left; take up the slack, then sweep the pole to the right, and repeat back and forth all the way.

3. WHIP OR BURNING

After the cast, reel in while raising your pole. When the pole is pointing up you can reverse the movement back to straight out in front of you, while reeling in for the entire time of this motion.

4. TWITCHING OR SHIMMY OR WAVING

Whatever position is comfortable to hold the pole while only wiggling or waving the tip of the pole will make the lure twitch, shimmy or wiggle slightly.

5. STOP 'N GO OR DYING

This is probably the easiest to do; whether you move the pole or not is up to you. The basis of this motion is reeling in, then stop and wait a little while, then reel in again.

Beware—all of these techniques have any number of variations and they may affect lures differently, so be prepared to try and try again until you feel comfortable doing these "pole positions." Good luck.

Mark Johnson
Tiskilwa, Illinois

A Monster Catch

Last May a friend of mine called and said that he was coming down and wanted to try his new boat and wondered if I would come along and help him get around in the backwaters and bayous in and around Ansley, Mississippi. How could I say no? So I told him to stop by my house and I'd be ready.

The next morning at 4:00 a.m. my friend showed up. I grabbed my fishing gear and my coffee and went to his truck, put my stuff in the back and away we went.

The sun had just started to lighten the sky when we pulled into the marina and the activity was everywhere. Boaters from all around the Gulf Coast area were sitting in line waiting to launch their boats. After an uneventful launch we headed out to the bay. As the boat turned the last curve and we headed out into the bay, the sun peeked over the edge of the world! The colors, brilliant orange and pinkish red, danced over the surface of the smooth bay waters, so wonderfully that they could bring a tear of joy to even the most manly of fishermen that day.

The day was warm and the tide was with us and after a few hours of some great action, the tide stopped and so did the fish. After awhile of no fish I decided to change location. I chose a place on the river that doesn't suffer from tide problems and we anchored out and took a look around.

I decided that, in light of the tides and such, if the fishing was slow I would practice (play with) my fly casting a bit. With a 6-pound leader on, I tied a froglike fly on the end and began to play out the line. I had learned to roll the line and make my fly pop the water without pulling my line out of the water. After a few rolls at the point of two bayous flowing into the river, my fly vanished and I thought I had lost it, so I began to reel my line back onto the reel when I noticed that my line was moving toward the boat! I quickly reeled until I felt a resistance on the end. I gave a little tug. WOW! The water exploded and the fight was on.

I knew that I could not get too rough with the fish (6-pound leader), it being a big fish. My friend yelled, "Whatcha' got there, Bud?" "Don't know," I yelled back and continued the fight. After about an hour (felt more like two) I had the brute tired enough to get it near the boat. When I saw what it was, a wicked thought crossed my mind (the saner of you people may not think it so funny).

I handed my friend the rod and told him to hold it for me. Before he could react I rolled off into the water and grabbed that fish and rolled him back into the boat. My friend took one look at him (a 6-foot, 40-pound alligator gar) and left the boat. I hung to the boat and burst out laughing and nearly drowned. When I looked at my friend his eyes were as big as plates. I had another round of laughter. When I could breathe again, I told him that I had just caught the thing in the very water he was now bobbing in. Another look of shock crossed his face and, whoosh-splash, he was back in the boat. My sides were beginning to ache and I decided to get back in the boat too. When I had gotten back in, my friend was perched up on the bow looking like a big old wet crow sitting on a fence.

I reached and grabbed the underside of the big fellow's gill plate and lifted him up. After some begging, I finally got my friend to help weigh and measure the fish. Then we lifted him back into the water and, with a little help, he regained his headway and went back to the depths from whence he came.

My friend has recovered from his shock and has since been back to fish. I have not encountered the monster again, but dream of the day that we might join in battle again.

James (Buddy) Smith
Columbia, Mississippi

Tackle Without Tangles

*T*o keep your hooks organized, if you have small plastic tackle boxes, Super-glue small magnets in the bottom of your hook compartments. This will keep the hooks from shifting and they will be tangle free.

Mike Goodman
Canyon Country, California

Fishing Follies

Perhaps it just wasn't
meant to be—
me a-fishin'
way up in a tree!
Lured by the docks,
the brush and the grass,
why that's not where
you'll find the BASS!
Castin' away,
careful—tree limb,
home for a bird
but not for a BREAM!
A pull and a tug,
a curse and a lurch,
muddied waters,
no more PERCH!
Perhaps I'll try
a different route,
another bait
to lure the TROUT!
Grab the net,
I've landed a SPECK!
I'm reelin' in—
what the HECK!

—Jane Prentice
Jonesville, Louisiana

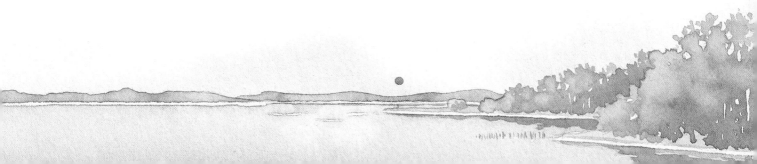

Keep on Fishin'

One Sunday morning, I went down to one of the local rivers. I had been trying this river out for some time, and believe me, the catfishing is somewhat awesome. There wasn't anything in particular about this day, and the weather was norm for this time (late spring). I had set up in this one little spot several times. What I would catch would be some bluegill, non-keepers (hand-fries), and perhaps a 2- or 3-pound catfish. One is enough for me.

I set up with two Johnson Telescopial Poles. As I sat there I reeled one of them in, using just wigglers. I noticed nothing had hit, so I set my reel to cast back in, and I cast a bit too high to clear the tree limb hanging out over the river. It got caught in some vines, so I tried to get my hook, line and sinker out of the mess.

At the same time, I heard something hit the water. I thought it might have been part of a vine that broke off, but after a couple of seconds of that thought, I looked down and noticed my other reel and rod were gone. I stopped what I was doing with the one hung in the vines and wandered over to the edge of the river bank to see if maybe I might have possibly kicked it in without knowing. But it wasn't anything like that. Something had made off with it.

Two weeks later, I had the weekend off. I went back, set up in the same spot (I really like this spot); I cast out, I let my bait lie at the bottom as usual for about 5 minutes. Later I began reeling and it felt like I had hooked into the tree limb lying in the river, so I pulled. Slowly but surely whatever I'd hooked came along. I reeled and tugged, and then I saw what looked like a part of a handle. I reeled in my lost rod and reel!

The Saturday morning when I had lost my pole, come Monday morning, met fellas, you know, shop talk before heading to get what's gotta be done. I had a chance to tell my little story of the one that got away (my rod and reel if you will).

Two Mondays after, in the afternoon, we're shooting the breeze and I had to tell them something that doesn't happen all the time. I showed the little trophy I pulled out of the river. Although 2 weeks had taken a toll lying at the bottom in the mud, I could only wonder what would I have hopefully pulled if I wasn't hanging in those vines.

If you love fishin'—keep on. I do.

Toney Miley
Tampa, Florida

Don't Give Up

No matter what the weather is, have a game plan, give it full effort, stick to your thoughts and don't give up. During cold fronts, the fish are still there and probably most are inactive, but some will strike. You just have to find them, catch them, photograph and release them.

A. Jim Heffner
Brodhead, Wisconsin

Flashy Fishing

Here's a quick and easy way to add a little flash to any presentation. Using a small split ring (size 1 works well), attach a small spinner blade to a small swivel (sizes 7 and 10 work well). Now slide about an 8-inch long section of plastic tubing (like aquarium or surgical tubing) over the free end of the swivel. Now just slip it on a hook, piercing the tubing, going through the eye of the swivel and back out the other side of the tubing. It works on any kind of lure to add a little extra attraction.

Jon Rasmussen
Menasha, Wisconsin

What Fishing is Really About

It was November, a beautiful sunny day, and I was on my way to Lake Pleasant, just outside Phoenix, Arizona, mid-afternoon on a weekday. The roads were quiet, my rods were rigged up and my secret bait was lying on the floor of my truck behind the driver's seat. I had fished this lake many times before for bass but due to a recent neck operation I had been forced to sell my bass boat.

For the last couple of months I had been fishing for carp. The first time I started off fishing for carp in this lake I used 15-pound-test line but something had taken the bait and snapped the line before I'd had the chance to set the hook. The next time out I had upgraded my line to 20-pound test, but the same thing continued to happen. I now had 30-pound monofilament on both reels and was ready for anything.

The lake was quiet. Every now and then the calm surface of the water was broken by a fish. I could not get the bait on my hooks fast enough. I cast out my rods and set them up on my homemade rod rests while my wife brought the folding table and chairs out of the truck and poured the coffee.

With one eye on my rods, I sat back and soaked in the beauty of the outdoors and made easy casual conversation with my wife—the stress of the office gradually leaving my body. I was hypnotized by a couple of eagles that kept circling endlessly around a grassy point without once flapping their wings.

Carp, by nature, are very skittish and by all accounts quite intelligent—they rank up there in the top six with catfish, I believe. The secret is not to mess around with the lines once they have been cast out. However, on this day I was beginning to feel that nothing was going to happen. For 50 minutes I sat there and not even a hint of a bite. They had even stopped breaking the surface of the water. Too much sun? Wind blowing in the wrong direction? Cold front coming in? Screwed up my bait? Bait fallen off my hooks?

I was about to bring in both lines and check the bait when suddenly one of the reels started screaming as the line was being stripped off. I knocked my wife, the coffee and the table everywhere in my haste to get to my rod before it became nothing but a memory. The fact that I almost ruptured myself in the process never crossed my mind as I grabbed the rod, set the hook and felt the resistance on the other end. I tried to adjust the drag to the point where I had a slight advantage but this in itself proved to be quite a challenge. The quality of my 10-foot rods was really put to the test. I could not speak. The power being exerted on my line was indescribable. After almost 10 minutes, I got the fish close enough to the bank to be able to determine that I had indeed caught a carp—the biggest mother I had ever seen. Then the beauty decided that she was going in the wrong direction, turned and took off again—another 50 yards off my spool. This action was better than any laxative.

After more than 15 minutes I managed to get the fish on to the bank and removed the hook from its mouth. The hook had been almost straightened out—another couple of minutes and I reckon I would have lost it. Using a spring balance (not the most accurate apparatus), I could see that she weighed about 42 pounds. My wife got the camera out as I posed with my trophy and then I released her back into the lake. With one flick of her tail, I was soaked and the fish was gone.

I helped put the table back up and got organized again and sat down for a while. I must have looked like a drunken idiot on St. Patrick's Day. I was trembling all over and I had a grin from ear to ear. What a feeling. I played the fight over and over again in my mind knowing that we both had won. I won because I got to hold the monster in my hands and the fish won because she was still swimming out there somewhere.

On the way home that evening I was talking to my wife about the photos and explained that she had to get them developed as soon as possible because no one would believe me unless I had the photos to back up my story. Calmly, my wife informed me that she had only taken one exposure. How I kept the truck on the road I will never know. (I will leave out the next part of the conversation).

When we arrived home, I immediately started bragging to my two sons about being the master fisherman of the house as I related the whole story. After I had completed my highly detailed adventure, my eldest son left the room and returned about 5 minutes later laughing hysterically. He had gone onto the Game & Fish

Fish website on the Internet and checked up on the State records. The Arizona State record for carp was set back in 1987 and was 38 pounds. I had just released a new state record and no one but my wife and I saw it—all I had was one undeveloped photo in the camera!

Fortunately, the solitary photo turned out all right.

Even though I do not have my name in the record books, that day is something I will never forget as long as I live. I've also come to realize that while setting records is very honorable, that is not what it is all about.

It's about getting out there, getting the lines into the water, getting in touch with nature, respecting others, and going home feeling revitalized—ready to take on the world again.

Remember, every hour spent fishing adds an hour to your life.

Keep those lines wet.

Keith Melrose
Austin, Texas

Homemade Lighted Bobber

To make a bobber that is visible at night as well as by day without spending loads of cash, just go to your local tackle shop and buy one of the glow sticks that fit on the tip of your rod. But instead of putting it on the tip of your rod, just snap it on one of those standing bobbers. It should hold tightly enough to fish with, but if not, just tie it on right above it so it still bobs.

Brandon Glassco
Sebree, Kentucky

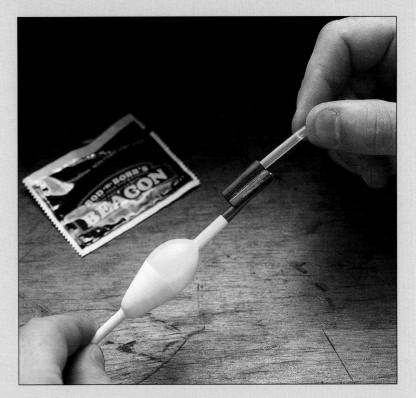

Ice Fishing Insights

My neighbor and I use a soft-side ice hut for our winter fishing. There were no rod holders provided in this hut. My neighbor built rod holders out of PVC pipe and sprinkler head shells.

Marlin Sigaty
Colorado Springs, Colorado

Full Moon Fishing

Try to plan fishing trips during full moon or new moon periods. A good share of my fish have been caught during the full moon.

A. Jim Heffner
Brodhead, Wisconsin

Floating Fish Basket

Here's how to make a "floater" for a fish basket. I have tried using a small inner tube. While this worked well, I found that the rubber either broke down and started leaking, or somehow became punctured. I then went to a local hobby store and purchased one of those Styrofoam rings used to make wreaths. I cut it in half, placed it around the top of the basket and glued it back together. Worked great … no more leaks!

Michael Leger
Albuquerque, New Mexico

Rod Protection

If you don't want to attach your hook to the eye of your pole because of getting scratches or because yours doesn't have anti-reverse, you can hold the lure against the pole and wrap a small piece of aluminum foil around it.

Chris Sloan
Lone Jack, Missouri

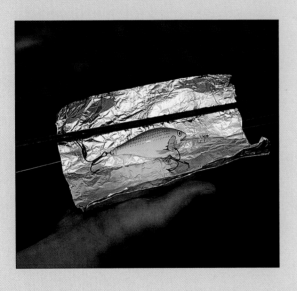

Bait for Bait

If you want to catch small fish and minnows to use for bait, mix:

3 teaspoons flour
1 teaspoon sugar
1 teaspoon water

Form the dough into small balls around the hook. It works best when using a cane pole because the dough doesn't hit the water so hard, and hence stays on the hook.

Timothy Koehn
Scooba, Mississippi

There, lying on the sandbar, where I had wanted to play so bad, were three of the biggest bass I had ever seen caught at one time. The fish weighed 7.25, 7.5 and 8 pounds. That day was never repeated, but we always had a great time together. I'll always remember the times we spent fishing together the most, and I'm so thankful that he cared enough about me to take me fishing.

—From "Thanks, Pop"

Bass Tales

Basszilla

It was an autumn day. I think it was during October. I was fishing while the sun was setting. I was bored and I still had a couple of hours since it was a half day at school. I was tired and thought of using a rattletrap, but I thought that I should try something new so I used a hula popper. I cast out the lure and sat down. Two minutes later I gave the popper a little tap. I could not see the lure because the sun was directly in front of me. My lure was blue, red, black and gray. I could barely make out the water. Then, I heard a little splash. "What was that," I thought to myself. BANG! A largemouth bass leaped with faith to cover the sun like an eclipse. My Shimano was at full drag and it still was taking out line. It took me 5 minutes to get BASSZILLA on shore. It was a 25-inch bass weighing an astonishing 8¼ pounds. I hope that this year I will have a baitcasting reel.

Aaron Mello
East Falmouth, Massachusetts

The One That Didn't Get Away

It was late one afternoon in early March. When I arrived home from my job, I told my wife I was going to our farm pond to do a little bass fishing. It was very quiet, except for a few early crickets chirping.

I began casting, working down the bank of the pond. I was fishing with a purple worm and had made several casts without any luck except for a few light taps. Almost ready to give up, I made a long cast, and was returning very slowly, when all of a sudden I felt a very unusual hard strike.

The bass took off very fast as I set the hook. He came up and jumped about 3 feet in the air. I almost lost my breath when I saw the size of this fish. I fought him for about 15 minutes, trying to wear him down. Suddenly, he made for a big wad of hydrilla grass and became hung. Now, I wondered, how was I going to save this big bass, since I was fishing from the bank and didn't have a boat to go to him? I laid my rod down on the bank with the bass still hung in the grass.

As fast as I could go, I ran back to the house to get a bow rake so I could try to rake him in. I tied a long rope to the rake and threw it in the wad of hydrilla. I began pulling. The huge fish, hydrilla and all, came forth.

A story hard to believe, but true. A 12-pound bass, caught by a rod and reel, a bow rake and a very nervous fisherman.

Nelson W. Taylor
Kinston, North Carolina

A Hard Day Fishing

During the summer I go fishing a lot. But there was this one day when everything I did was wrong.

I woke up at 6:15 and got ready to go fishing with my friend down below Bilby Dam. When we got there I got at least five knots in my line before I even caught a fish. The fish weren't really biting that good that day either.

We moved to the next fishing spot and caught a few. Of course, who got hung on rocks, cut a finger and got knots in their line? Me.

By the time we got to the second-from-last fishing hole I was ready to go home, but I didn't. I might have had 20 feet of line. When I got there I had caught maybe two fish, and my friend, 10 or so.

On the way to the last fishing hole I cut my knee open. When we got to the last fishing hole I had about 10 feet of line left. I switched bait from a blue Little Lucy to a white Little Lucy. I threw it in a few times before I even got a strike. I caught a few fish, then I threw it in for the last time before we left. I started to reel it in when my line started going from side to side; then my pole jerked up and down like crazy, so I jerked up as hard as I could. I hooked it. It took out all my line (which was about 10 feet) and I almost lost the whole rod and reel, the fish was moving so fast. I don't know how I kept from losing the fish. I got the fish in about halfway, then it

jumped at least 2 feet out of the water and splashed water all over us. I reeled in a little more and it did it again. That time I could tell what it was—it was a smallmouth bass. When I finally got it in I measured and weighed it. It measured 18½ inches, and weighed 3 pounds. I released it so I might be able to catch it again this spring or summer. So far, it is the second largest fish my friends and I have caught.

Brandon Wright
Woodlawn, Virginia

Cats, Bass and Louie

Most stories are about the one that got away. Not this one. This is one morning worth a million smiles. We are at Findley State Park, Wellington, Ohio. It's 4 a.m., it's my first time here, it's total darkness—no flashlights or lanterns here—those would get you shot in some places, I'm told by Louie. "This isn't Lake Erie Edgewater," he says (the only place I've ever fished at up to this point). A kid sitting on the rocks all night with a lantern and worms, sinkers, hooks, other tackle gear, a radio, beverage and munchies.

He says, "It's all by feel and sound, and all you need is a jitterbug. The rest is how you work it."

With that he casts away, and begins to work it till I hear this percolator noise, working his jitterbug across the top of the water, listening to the percolator popping sound, when above it all I hear this huge, loud POP and water-splash sound. I hear a faint whisper, "2-pounder," as he's still reeling in. I'm not paying any attention at all to my lure right about now, listening to Louie's line and reel.

Then I hear this sound like a huge rock dropped in the water. "Kerplunk." Next thing I know I feel like I'm being tugged by a freight train. The reel drag starts to sing, I'm reeling like mad; I tighten the drag and keep on reeling. Louie has landed his and I'm still reeling. He comes over to where I am and says, "Hey, you need a hand with that 10-pound cat?"

"Cat??? Cool!" Reeling like mad now, it becomes very obvious it is a cat. It feels like I'm dragging a ton of bricks across the bottom. Finally close enough, feeling my way, still in the dark, reaching down, feeling around till I get hold of it, dragging it out on the shore, not sure exactly how big it is yet.

All I know at this point of the game is, it's dark and "I GOT IT." I don't know what I've got, but I know the "I GOT IT" feeling running through me. You know that feeling I mean, "the one everyone gets when they hook a fish, admit it or not."

Well, after managing to get it landed and carried in the dark away from the water, I pulled out my little key-chain light. I shined it on what I had reeled in and, sure enough, it was not only a cat, but a channel cat with beautiful spots, silver-blue shiny body, long whiskers, huge fins, big ol' mouth just gnawing away at my lure, both hooks set in it. I had a hand scale in the tackle box.

Just then Louie walks over, looks down and says, "See, a 10-pound cat, I told ya." "I dunno how, but it's a cat." "You must have crossed its nest area," he says, scratching his head. I asked, "How'd you know?" He says, "It sounded like a brick hit the water, right? And see what you reeled in? Now turn off that light, get your lure back in the water and get some of these," as he holds up his 2-pound largemouth bass. With that he walks back over to the water, releases his fish and says to it, "Send me back your great-great-granddad."

I start to remove the hooks from Old Silver and get this fish back in the water. Yes, I said get it back in the water. I never keep my first fish caught each year. Its sorta something I just always do. I release the first one I catch.

Well, Louie darn near fainted when I did that, but he understood after I said, "Go lay them eggs, Momma." I had seen this cat had a huge fat belly, tight with eggs soon to be laid.

Now, Louie is already back at it—reel, pop, pause, reel, pop, pause, POP-SPLASH! He has another one. I hear him say, "Black 10! This one's breakfast!" He got it in the bucket and casts again. After five fish and less than an hour's work he had his breakfast, and for all of 'em he would call off numbers like at a roulette table. When I weighed his fish, all of 'em were what he called off—1, 10, 4, 5, 7 pounds.

Remember I promised this story was worth a million smiles? Here's why—the reason I was catching fish other than largemouth bass was because I was putting a worm on the jitterbug, casting and moving it around, treating it like a bobber.

I thought if it had a hook you baited it, right? Fancy bobber with more hooks for more worm equals big fish! I caught a catfish, so it seemed to be working for me, I thought to myself.

Well, what did I know. I was a young kid then. I had never even heard of a jitterbug till right then, yet I did manage to get a bass that morning after I reeled in 10 small bluegills that were feasting on my fancy jitterworm, but the 5-pounder I did get when I figured it out was a

good start for my first-ever largemouth bass. Today, I'm looking forward to teaching my 8-year-old son what a jitterbug is, even with a worm on it for those days when the fish just aren't biting and nothing else works.

Now we've added a Polaroid 320 mini digital cam to the tackle box—tiny, light and simple to use, and it hooks up to your PC. Photos of the fishing world through "New Eyes" soon to come; my son's already asking if I own an underwater cam, like in the game Trophy Bass on our PC, so he can see them when they take his hook and not let them steal his bait. Why didn't we have that as kids? I bet we would have lost less bait.

Till our next line comes out to you, find someone to share memories like this with, and take the time to enjoy what little time you have with them.

Thanks Louie I hope heaven has a big enough wall for all your trophy "great-grand-daddy bass." One of the best friends a guy could have; thanks for being one of mine. I'll never forget ya.

Merlin Novak
Cleveland, Ohio

Lure Retrieve Technique

Although I consider myself mainly a soft-bait angler, one of my favorite lures for use in shallow waters and ponds is the spinner. I use almost exclusively Mepps lures because I like their design and action. I generally use sizes 1 through 3 in the "Aglia" line although other sizes and models also work well.

One thing I have discovered in recent years is that fish, especially bass, seem to really respond to this type of lure when I begin retrieving a split second before the lure hits the water. Do not allow it to sink! This gives the fish an element of surprise, thinking that a bug has hit the water and has decided to skim its way across or just below the surface. The action of the spinning blade draws the fish's attention and they almost immediately begin going after it.

Because you are reeling in at a moderate rate, the hookset is almost automatic, much like a larger safety-pin-shaped spinnerbait. I have even clipped one or two of the hooks off the treble to give it more of a semi-weedless design where needed. I have landed bass in the 1- to 3-pound range using this method. It also works well with panfish!

Remember, always gear your line weight to the size of the lure! Try it. This is action fishing at its best.

Lin McDowell
Canton, Ohio

The Cutting Edge

Perfect conditions! We hear about these kinds of days occurring in the life of a bass fisherman. So what do you do with these conditions? The answer is really quite simple—go fishin'!

Here is the scenario of a day I had with "perfect conditions." The time was when late spring turns to early summer. The location was in the northeastern part of the country. Now, keep in mind that a "big bass" is relative to where you live. In northern waters, a 6-pounder is as much of a trophy as a 12-pounder in Florida, California, Texas or any of the other big bass meccas.

However, many of us don't have the means to travel to such places. What I did have was a light, warm breeze, partially cloudy skies and water temperatures between 62 and 68°F.

I started out by grabbing my tackle box, fishing poles, a net with a 30-inch handle, some lunch and my 9-year-old son who was, incidentally, already waiting outside in the Jeep.

Our plan was to head for a nearby river whose current flows through a steep-banked area of heavy cover and trees. The shore depth drops quickly from about 3 feet to 15. This was big bass territory and an excellent place for bank fishing. Its remote location was only accessible by a footpath down through the woods.

I strapped on my Chicago Cutlery 6-inch fillet knife and sheath. We grabbed the gear and started down the pathway to the river. As we approached the water, we saw a beautiful blue heron fly overhead and the sounds of various birds and wildlife greeted us as we entered their domain. My son found a grassy knoll that overlooked a quiet pool, which had an undercut bank. He was fishing a live worm and plastic float setup. I positioned myself to his left and down the bank. The area was a side channel with current that moved into a backwater area. In back of us, up the hill, was the treeline where we entered and set down our extra poles, lunch and net on the grass. The light breeze carried the scent of spruce trees and wildflowers. The sky had turned a vibrant blue, dotted with many large and fluffy white clouds.

My gear choice was a 7-foot medium-heavy baitcasting rod with 17-pound-test line. I was fishing a torpedo propbait in a drift-and-twitch technique. I would cast to my right and let it drift past me to my left. My propbait choice comes into play in situations where the plug can drift behind stumps and limbs. If I can get it into a tight spot and hold the bait, the current works the propeller and the lure begins bobbing around. I've also fished a 7- or 8-inch plastic worm with a small pegged weight this way and had great results.

My son's bobber went down and he yelled, "Got one!" He pulled in a real nice yellow perch. He followed that with a smaller one and then a bluegill. As his fish count rose, so did his level of expertise! After each of his casts, he would boldly say, "You better go up the hill and get that net! Don't worry, Dad, it's early, you'll get something!"

On my fourth cast the current took the bait behind a tree limb and into a spot I had hoped for. As the propeller turned, I twitched the bait erratically and, bang! I set the hook and the bass went airborne! I quickly pulled the fish away from the pocket and out of the cover. My medium-heavy rod was the key in directing the fish out of the cover. I pulled the fish up the bank and it fell off the hook, landing at my feet. It was a nice 2½- to 3-pound largemouth. I quickly released the fish and made another cast. My son yelled, "You're lucky it landed at your feet. You should get that net."

Using the same method, I managed to land two more 2-pounders. Both of them fell off at my feet as well. My "fishing coach" had numerous things to say! He had caught two more bluegills.

Action slowed down, so I switched to an 8-inch plastic worm. I was very careful of my placement and drift technique. I let the bait follow the cover and drift close to the bank area around a fallen tree. As the bait settled, I twitched lightly. The quiet river sound was disrupted by a loud splash as my line went tight! I set the hook and after a few flights over the branches, I landed a nice 3½-pounder. After setting the bass free, I made two more casts. The first cast brought in a 2-pounder, the second got caught in the fallen tree, and the fish and line were lost. I quickly set up my line again with the very same type of plastic worm and cast back to the same area, hoping for the current to be kind to me.

My fishing coach watched intently as he fished. I made three more casts and finally, the bait drifted further into the fallen tree. The area near the bank seemed

a little deeper. It looked like it could be a deep undercut bank. I let the bait sink and drift more before I began to twitch it lightly. The breeze had let up and the quiet was suddenly disrupted when I felt my line get extremely heavy. I set the hook, and it felt like I had driven the hook into a submerged log. I could hardly feel movement. Suddenly, the "log" started moving upriver!

My fishing coach quickly froze at the sight of the tension on my 7-foot pole. He then yelled, "Dad! If that's a fish, I hope your drag is set right!" I directed the movement away from the cover. Suddenly, the fish's direction turned and headed back toward me. I was sure glad my reel had a high gear ratio. I was really crankin' as the speed picked up. Just then, the surface erupted and we caught sight of the beast! It was a horse with fins! My son dropped his fishing pole and ran toward me. The horse dove and tried to head upriver again. I directed it back. He surfaced again, as if he had wings. It seemed to fly 2 feet above the water! The fish bulldogged and then came to the surface once again, but not quite jumping clear. We were now able to see the size of him. We saw what was left of the 8-inch worm hanging from the mouth of a largemouth bass that had to be in the 6½- to 7½-pound range, no problem! This fish was BIG!

After more fighting and traveling up and down the river, I directed the fish to the shallow water, down the steep bank directly in front of me. Suddenly the bass rolled sideways and then the horror hit us—the fish was no longer attached to the hook and mashed worm! It was actually being quite still. I quickly dropped my pole and reached for the net—it wasn't there! My fishing coach quickly said, "Dad, it's up the hill near the woods, remember?" As fast as you can say, "One more cast," I reached to my side to draw my knife. My thought was to jab the knife into the sand above the fish to prevent his rolling into the deeper water. This would give me time to grab him. But the knife would not come out because the sheath was riding up. I grabbed the sheath quickly with my left hand as I grabbed the knife with my right. I felt a funny sensation in my left hand, but didn't pay much attention to it. I fell to the ground, onto my stomach, to get closer. I drew back the knife and the fish started slightly moving around. As I looked at the water and that big ol' horse, I noticed the water getting red. Suddenly, the fish decided the visit had been long enough. As the blade zoomed through the air toward the fish, he rolled and disappeared into the deeper water! My fishing coach stared in amazement as the water turned a deeper crimson, and I suddenly realized I was in pain.

I knew I had lost the "Loch Ness Monster," but that pain was superceded by the pain in my left hand. As I got up onto my feet, I glanced down and noticed that two fingers on my left hand were cut open and bleeding profusely. In my haste to grab my knife, I had unknowingly sliced my fingers. My son handed me the fisherman's crying towel and I wrapped my hand until we could get the first aid kit. It looked worse than it actually was. As we walked up the hill to get our lunches, my son said, "Dad, that was sure a really big fish!" I turned and kicked the nearest tree as I replied, "You ain't kidding!"

Well, we sat down on the grass to eat lunch and enjoy a day of "perfect conditions." I turned to my son and said, "Coach, this day has truly been 'The Cutting Edge' of bass fishing."

Dennis J. Fallo
Alfred, Maine

Thanks, Pop

When I was 3 years old, my dad took me fishing for the first time. We would bass fish from a small aluminum boat on whatever ponds he could get permission to fish or by paying a small fee to the landowner.

I wanted to do all that fancy casting and reeling like he did, but he had other ideas in mind that probably saved us many a trip to get hooks removed from us both. To make me content, he gave me two rods to use, saying that I had a better chance to catch a fish than he did with just one. He also knew that if we did manage to dodge the hooks I would be throwing, I would never last casting and give out on him too soon.

My two rods had Zebco 33 reels and he had rigged them for me with big round plastic bobbers, a swivel with a snelled hook, and a big 4-inch shiner. He would drive 30 miles out of town to the nearest place that sold these, just for me to use. I sat in the back of the boat with my two rods opposite each side trailing behind the boat, while he was up front with his paddle and casting his spinnerbait. He loved spinnerbait fishing and I would watch in amazement at how he could put that bait anywhere he wanted it to go.

I remember catching fish, though usually not as big as his. I was getting better and he was allowing me to cast on my own. On my fourth birthday he took me fishing and I caught my first 3-pound bass, all by myself, with him netting the fish for me. It was great; I was finally catching something bigger than the bait I was using, and the fishing fever had taken over me.

By the time I was 6, I was putting more fish in the boat than he was, but on one particular day that I'll always remember, we had only one fish. I had gotten bored and impatient, and wanted to go to the bank and play on the sandbar that was on the side of the pond. Finally after my persistence and my dad realizing it was either that or take me home, he gave in and we got out so I could play for a while. Dad rigged his baitcaster as he had my rods and threw all three out as far as he could off the sandbar.

I was determined to play in the sand no matter what, and no sooner had he thrown the last rod out, than the first one's bobber went under. With my back to the water I heard him grunt as he set the hook. He always grunted on a hookset so I knew what was going on without even looking. But this time was different. After a minute I heard him grunt again and heard the excitement in his voice telling me to "get the other rod because the bobber on it is under, too!" As I turned

around, I saw a huge bass flopping up on the bank, the hook still in its mouth, and my dad madly fighting another fish. I ran and grabbed the last rod left in the water, pulled back to set the hook and held on. Just about the time I thought about either letting go of the rod or going swimming, my dad took the rod from me. I don't know if it was to save me or the rod from going into the water, but either way I was glad he did and I didn't have to make that decision.

There, lying on the sandbar, where I had wanted to play so bad, were three of the biggest bass I had ever seen caught at one time. The fish weighed 7.25, 7.5 and 8 pounds. Needless to say my dad loved the sandbar and took me back there on several other occasions, so I could "play" even though I would tell him I didn't want to play.

That day was never repeated, but we always had a great time together. When I was 8 years old I landed my first bass over 8 pounds without his help and was getting pretty good with the baitcaster. For some reason he took my rods with shiners and allowed me to try and do all the fancy casting and reeling that I so admired him for doing. My dad was the biggest influence on my entry into the world of fishing and, if it had not been for him, I might not ever have caught the fishing fever that I have today.

My dad left about 3 years ago to go be with the Lord, and though I miss him now, I know that he's already found us another place and is waiting on me to join him so that we can fish together again. We spent 28 years together fishing and learned a lot from each other. With all the influence that this man had in my life, I'll always remember the times we spent fishing together the most, and I'm so thankful that he cared enough about me to take me fishing.

• The tips from my story would be: Parents, take your children fishing. They may like it, they may not, but either way, they will never forget it. And sons or daughters, get your parents to take you fishing, or better yet, if you can, take them. You'll be glad you did.

J. Kevin Edwards
Danville, Alabama

Bonding Memories

It was a hard day at work, but I wasn't about to let anything come between a nice relaxing time at the pond and me. I rushed home to get my gear ready for the eventful trip. As I walked in the door, I heard my wife say something to me. Her words did not register because my thoughts were on fishing. The only phrase to catch my attention was, "And you have to watch Zachary" (our 14-month-old baby).

My mouth dropped! As I mentioned earlier, I wasn't about to let anything come between my fishing time and me on this day. I decided to take him along, a decision I would never forget. It would prove to be quite a "bonding" adventure.

A beautiful fall day awaited our presence. As I walked to the shore of the pond, my son squirmed in the backpack carrier. I was a little hesitant to fish in this manner. It would be horrible to hook my son and go home with a 20-pounder. He was surprisingly cooperative after I gave him a fake worm to play with. I would catch an occasional bass and show him the fish, which kept him content. Throwing a few casts and walking to another spot was the procedure I followed. I did this until we hiked around the whole 4-acre pond.

On one of our last stops I cast my fake worm into an edge of a weedbed. I slowly reeled my line in and saw a nice bass following my worm. The back dorsal fin rose right out of the water. My heart was pounding, but I kept my composure and let the worm fall back in front of his mouth. He sucked it in and took off. I set the hook and the fight was on. I was using my ultralight rod because I hadn't caught a fish larger than 15 inches at that pond all summer long. My son had brought me luck!

I fought the fish for awhile and tired him out. This brought me to another dilemma. I had no net, so how was I going to get him out of the water? If I leaned over, my son would fall out of his pack. My line was also too thin for me to

pull him up the bank. I ended up doing the splits and grabbed the fish by the mouth. The fish was over 22 inches long; the largest bass I had ever caught! Throughout the rest of the fall we fished this way, creating a "bonding time" with two of my favorite passions: family and fishing! So here's my simple tip:

• Invest in a backpack carrier to create many fishing memories with your young children.

David L. Mielke
Hemlock, Michigan

Crazy About Fishing

My wife does not understand, and cannot comprehend, my passion for fishing. She is very understanding and supportive of this "obsession" as she calls it, and my love for the outdoors. But she just doesn't quite see this perfect picture I paint for her, each time I share with her my experiences and the excitement of my anticipation for the next fishing trip. I mean, "Why would anyone in their right mind get out of bed on their only day off from work (earlier than usual) just to go fishing?" Sound familiar?

The clock was set for 4:30 a.m. As I watched the minutes tick down to 4:19, I turned the alarm off before it had a chance to wake up the whole house. The night before was spent doing the "old routine" that I grew up doing since my dad blessed me with this incurable fishing desire that I have. This consists of checking the lines, retying knots, organizing the tackle box and getting everything together for the next day's fishing trip. "Be prepared ahead of time," is what my dad always stressed to me, "so when you're on the water, you can utilize your time for fishing, not preparing to fish." I always looked forward to that "old routine" and still do to this day. It is as much a part of fishing as the fishing itself.

Everything is laid out the night before and dressing is done in the dark to prevent any disturbance to those with better sense, who would rather be sleeping. As I try to quietly leave the bedroom, the silence is broken by a sweet gentle grumble (as my wife sums up exactly how she feels about me and my fishing in two simple words) proclaiming "You're crazy." I kiss my beautiful wife on the forehead and think to myself, "Yes, I guess I am," considering the alternative of staying in bed with her. But, nevertheless—I'm Going Fishing!

Just as daylight is beginning to break, I'm sliding my small aluminum boat known as "The Aluminum Pie Pan" into my favorite fishing pond. The small boat bobbles back and forth as I leave the bank and head to my favorite fishing spot. I've caught a lot of bass from this honey hole, but none over 2 to 3 pounds, and have lost a couple of 4- to 5-pounders. The largest bass known caught from here was over 7.5 pounds, but even larger ones are known to roam these waters.

It's late May and the fish are post spawn. I'm using my favorite white buzz bait as the early morning fog rises off the water. The water boils behind the bait as a small bass comes to the surface to see what all that noise is about. He thinks twice and goes back to his hiding place just outside of the weeds.

A few more casts and I've reached my favorite spot, slowly working the bait through the weeds and around objects in the water. I throw across and past a small point protruding into the water. It's just a small break in the shoreline structure, nothing major, but just enough to make a difference. Then, all of a sudden, the early morning silence and the stillness of the water are disrupted by such an explosion, I thought an alligator had left the bank, until I felt a sudden impact and resistance on my retrieve.

Then I saw the fish as he made an attempt to break water and get rid of this thing that he had just taken into his huge mouth. The rod had such a bow in it I wondered if it might snap in two, leaving me nothing but the handle. I hear the zing of my drag, and I'm trying to keep the fish on. I finally get to see more of him as he tries another attempt to free the hook from his massive jaws and lifts his head out of the water, exposing half of his body as he does a fancy tail walk on the water.

I played him to the boat, then lifted him out of the water and admired him. Removing the hook from his mouth, I estimated his size at 7 to 8 pounds. I quickly put him into my aerated Coleman cooler live well for further weighing and measurement later and got back to fishing. I positioned the boat in the same exact location as before and made another cast. As the buzz bait reached the same spot there was another explosion, not as big or vicious as the last, but a good strike, anyway. After a brief battle I landed this fish and estimated it at 4 to 5 pounds.

Fishing for another hour produced only a couple of small bass and, with the combination of gusting winds and my curiosity to examine these trophy bass more closely, forced me to the bank for an official weigh-in. My trusty De-Liar amazed me as the big fish pushed the scale readout past 9 pounds and measured 26 inches in length. The second weighed 5 pounds and measured almost 22 inches. Wow, two nice fish on back-to-back

casts with the 9-pounder being my biggest bass ever.

No one showed up for the final weigh-in. No cameras. No spotlights. No crowd. No reporters. Not even anyone to photograph this trophy with me. But I still have the memory of a lifetime and, after thinking over what my wife had said to me that morning, I came to the conclusion that if insanity is measured by the amount of enjoyment you receive from doing something you love, then I guess I am indeed crazy.

J. Kevin Edwards
Danville, Alabama

Hooked

Keeping up with my father's long stride required a much faster pace for this 6-year-old, as I followed him down the walk in front of my grandparents' farmhouse and across the road and through the gate at the neighbor's pasture. The sound of locusts was intense and the air was filled with an abundance of flying insects. It was a hot, late afternoon in the summer of 1954, and grasshoppers sprang from weed to weed to escape the thrashing foliage as we trod into the meadow.

A hundred yards across the field, we entered into the welcomed shade of the tall elms and willows that lined Fishing Creek and marked our spot on the bank. It was a popular fishing hole, obviously evident by the barren ground and the forked sticks left protruding from the sandy soil by anglers to support their fishing poles. Here, we would spend the rest of the afternoon attempting to fill a stringer with the ever-evasive bass.

Relatively new to fishing, and having only caught tiny bluegills on previous excursions, my techniques were yet unpolished and clumsily applied. However amateurish my skills, I persisted in that silent anticipation felt by all anglers—the landing of the Big One.

My attempts to secure a worm to my hook were met by violent resistance from the red earth creature. However, after several attempts to duplicate my father's technique, I managed to precariously affix the bait to the hook and cast it into the water. This ritual would be repeated many times that afternoon, as the fish were picking my hook faster than I could bait up. If bluegills could talk, they would have thanked me for the banquet that I catered all afternoon. Yet, they lurked about, awaiting another of the gourmet red worms to be served.

Across the creek and beyond the railroad tracks, a steep hill lies in wait of the sun's passing. The afternoon would soon be replaced by evening as the sun was now glaring off the water and into my face. Its cresting of the hill rendered a golden glow over the valley. The long hours without a catch had transformed my anticipation into melancholy and having lost my last worm I was now reduced to oscillating my empty hook in the water just a few feet from the shore. Suddenly, I was nearly relieved of my fishing rod by a strong jerk on the line. "I got one!" I screamed, jerking my catch onto the ground behind me.

My father, who was just a few yards away, retrieved his line and joined my celebration. His day of fishing, to this point, was only fractionally better than mine. A wide grin spread across his face, as he always rejoiced in his children's successes. "That's a nice one!" he exclaimed. A quick measurement revealed my first bass to be 9 inches.

Our return to the house was met with much heralding and soon followed by a photograph of me and my trophy. Needless to say, I was one proud 6-year-old, having graduated, that day, from bluegills to the larger gamefish and on an empty hook. Given the event of that day, I pondered, "Who really gets hooked when a fish is caught?"

M. Edward Wyatt
Colliers, West Virginia

A Special Gift

Three years ago now I wrote a "thank you" letter to an Amish gentleman friend of mine, Amos Miller. Amos ran a small business just east of a small country town here in northern Indiana. He is a quiet man, built like a lumberjack and as gentle as they come.

Among the many items sold in his store, one corner carried fishing tackle. Along with other baits were a dozen colors of a lure called "Bass Killer." This plastic worm bait is a big hit with me as it catches bass when no other lure will. I buy them by the card and in about three colors.

What's so special about this bait is that it's hand-poured in a wooden mold that was hand-carved by an Amish gentleman in the Shipshewana area some years ago. His name was Stutzman, and that's where the nickname of Stutzie came from.

"Stutzie" baits have a little anise oil mixed in with the plastic. Two gold aberdeen hooks on 8-pound-test line is the leader. Then each of these baits is hand-tied and packaged by family members. The business has changed hands over the last few years and the lures are now made by a younger Amish man in the Nappanee, Indiana, area. The last I knew, these folks make over 65,000 per year in over 30 colors.

I have fished this lure for many years, and have found it very effective in clearwater lakes. The way I like to fish this bait is by using it rigged Carolina style. The best way to identify how to fish this bait is to "do nothing." Simply cast it out and let it sink down to the bottom, then just move the bait as slow as possible. Of course a good breakline is helpful.

But I'm getting ahead of myself. I want to share with you the "thank you" letter that I sent Amos. What follows hopefully will give you an idea how I feel about Amos Miller. I need to set the stage, though, as to why Amos sent me a box of "Stutzie's" in the first place.

I had stopped by Amos's store one Christmas season with a Christmas gift of English walnuts just to tell Amos how much I had enjoyed his friendship over the past few years; nothing more, just a thank you. The very next week here comes a UPS truck backing in my driveway with a small box. The return address on the box told me it was from Amos. Rushing into the house to see what was inside the box, I found it contained a dozen "Stutzie's" baits of different colors. What a surprise. But how do I say thank you to Amos for this generous gift?

I never sent a thank you card to an Amish gentleman before. It didn't feel just right to me. Then it came to me. Why not write a short note on counting the days till the ice will be off the lakes and the water starts to warm up. So here's my story:

Dear Amos Miller,

Just a note of thanks for the surprise package I received last week via UPS. I thank you so very much, and of course you know you did not need to do that.

I'm already looking forward to springtime when I'll be able to get back on a nearby lake some lightly overcast morning with just a hint of a ripple on the lake's surface. Ah yes, I can see it all now.

The sun is just peeking through a small opening in the overcast coming through the tops of the trees. I'm ready to fish. The hardest thing now is to pick out a bait to use. I decide to start right off with a Stutzie. What color? Let's see, purple will do just fine. I'll just tie one on my 8-pound-test line and we're ready. First cast, right over by those lily pads. Can you see them? They sit out just a little more than some of the others. I want to take my time now. Easy does it, there it goes, the line leaving my spinning reel making a soft sound, as the cast reaches its target, just in the right spot near the lily pads, with an ever-so-quiet entry into the water.

Now let the Stutzie do its thing. Sinking ever so slow, down it goes to the bottom. Now just let it lie there for a bit. I engage the reel and take up a little slack; easy now, not too fast, remember it's a do-nothing bait. Time now to give the bait a little movement, not too much, just an inch, 2 at the most, wait again.

Boy, what a great day I'm thinking, looking around noticing the hues coming through the trees. It's easy to let one's mind drift off on a morning like this so I had better mind my line.

Then it happens … the line starts to move, or was that the boat that moved with the air movement? Not sure. There it goes again, this time no

Slingshot Toss

When in tight spots where you must get your bait in a small area where it won't get snagged and you can still catch that fish, I use a technique which I call the "Slingshot Toss." First, take your bait and hold its lowest hooks by the side. Make sure you have enough line to reach about halfway down your pole. Second, pull back the bait while holding the slack button down, so you don't let it slip. Aim the bait as if it were in a slingshot. Let the bait go and, right before it passes the end of your pole, release the slack button. When you have your bait in the desired spot, use your favorite technique to catch whatever species of fish you are fishing for.

Anthony Webb
Bogue Chitto, Mississippi

doubt about it … that's a bass bite and he's starting to take line. "Set the hook," I tell myself. "Set the hook or you're going to lose him," this time aloud. The hook is set, the fight is on.

Man, what a fish. He's taking line off the reel and moving off to the right, heading back into the pads. "Oh no you don't, Big Guy," again out loud, as I put a little pressure on him to wear him down a bit. Just then he makes a run to open water. Better check the drag, I'm thinking; not too tight and not too loose.

Here he comes, headed right for the boat. Reel, man, reel in the slack. That's it, he's now back on the line. Then the rod bends way over as he nears the boat and heads for the bottom. Now he comes to the surface next to the boat. I ask myself, is he ready to be taken? Still looks a little green.

With rod lifted high and getting down on my knees I reach over the side of the boat. There he is in all his glory, one largemouth bass in hand. What a great gamefish. He'll go 5 pounds, I say to myself as I lean back to catch my breath. He took the top hook. Nothing beats spring fishin'.

I've had my fun, so back he goes for perhaps another time, for I now know where he lives; besides, he's just too nice a largemouth to catch only once. There he goes, no worse for wear, "See ya later," I said out loud, "See ya later."

Amos, I guess you know I'll be using those Stutzies next spring in a little over 90 days from now. Thanks again for the package.

Happy New Year to You and Yours,
Jim Kehr

That's my story. I have fished Stutzies for a long time and when fishin' for largemouth bass when times are slow I'll put on a Stutzie and catch bass when no other lure will work.

When you try a Stutzie, fish it slowly on a clear body of water. Just work it on or near the bottom, then hang on. I've boated well over 40 bass in less then 5 hours when other anglers have just a few.

Happy fishing, and don't forget to release the big guys so they can grow to fight another day. They are the future in bass fishing, you know. Good luck.

Jim Kehr
Middlebury, Indiana

Beating the Monday Blues

efore I stepped out onto the dock this fine morning, I stopped to enjoy the beauty before me. The sun was breaking the horizon, the water in Lake Gibson appeared dark and enchanting; it was as smooth as glass. The air was brisk. This was truly a sight to behold.

Although I was dressed in a suit and tie, and had to leave for work in approximately 4 minutes, I took my time walking the 123 feet to reach my pole. I was a little optimistic today, as this was the perfect time of year to catch a trophy fish.

Each night I throw a line off the end of my dock with a 4-inch shiner on it and put my spinning rod in a holder so that a fish cannot pull it in. I have checked it daily for the past 6 weeks with only a 14-inch catfish to show for my time and effort. However, my bait was missing on several occasions, my line was snapped once, and even wrapped around the underwater dock supports another time, by what appeared to be a very smart fish.

Nevertheless, I thought that today could very well be the day. As I approached the end of the pier, full of excitement and anticipation, I searched for my chartreuse cork. It was nowhere in sight. My heart started pounding as I reached for my spinning rod, knowing full well that this was the moment I had been waiting for. Slowly I reeled in the slack line and then set the hook with authority. The fish was heavy and full of fight. He responded by running for the deep water in the middle of the lake, taking line with him.

Full of excitement and thoroughly enjoying this "adventure," I looked around me to see if anyone was watching; a neighbor, an earlybird fisherman, anyone. I wanted to share this experience with someone, but it was only me and the mighty fish. I wondered what kind it was and whether I would, in fact, ever see it. It had stripped out over 80 yards of line by this time and was showing no signs of weakening.

I knew I would be late for my ride to work this day, but somehow this was not important to me. I was caught up in an adventure that would remain a part of me for many years to come.

The fish came in grudgingly at first, but all at once he swam straight for me at full speed. I reeled as fast as I could and caught up with him about 20 feet from the dock, when he suddenly turned and made his second attempt for deep water. He was a true fighter for sure. I grasped my rod with a firm grip, keeping the tip high, and just hung on as he continued his surge. When he had gained 20 yards of line he stopped to rest. I took quick advantage, pumping my rod tip up and down, regaining as much line as I could.

The fish still had not shown himself, but I felt him weakening, so I reached for my net from the seat behind

me. Suddenly my adversary made an unexpected move; he came to the top, showing himself for the first time, made a violent swirl and dove straight for the bottom. I felt lucky to still have hold of this mighty foe, as this tactic caught me completely by surprise, in what appeared to me to be his final attempt for freedom. The fish slowed down and I could feel he was tiring. I put pressure on him, maneuvering him to the end of the dock where I was kneeling with the net in my left hand. He came in grudgingly, diving and swirling, but after three short dives he turned over on his side, admitting defeat.

I swiftly slipped the net under the fish and triumphantly lifted him onto the dock, where I stood for a moment admiring the striped bass, a fish new to the freshwater lakes of Florida. Then, realizing I would be late catching my ride to work, I ran down the dock and rushed into the house, where my wife, 13-year-old daughter and 9-year-old son greeted me at the door. They explained that they saw me running down the dock with my fishing pole in one hand and the bulging net in the other, and came to investigate.

Leaving the fish with instructions to put him on ice until I could take his vital statistics, I ran to my car and sped the 3 miles to catch my ride to work. Luckily, he was just pulling out of his driveway when I got there, as he was running late also.

I could never have planned a better way to start a Monday morning.

Paul Hawks
Auburndale, Florida

Crankbait Preservation

Here's a tip that helps keep those 5- to 10- dollar crankbaits from decorating the bottom of your fishing areas. Cut two pieces of thin, but stiff, wire about 6 inches long each. Now, place the crankbait in a vise to hold it still. Wrapping it in a rag preserves the paint job and keeps it from getting crushed. Next heat up the end of each wire and insert it into the leading edge of the bait's diving lip so that they are centered about ¼ inch apart. Curl the wires so that they extend outward and downward from the front of the bait, and trim to desired length. Last thing to do is take a couple of casts and retune the bait to run straight. This works best on deep-diving baits where the lip extends almost straight out from the bait. The wires run along the bottom like a bottom bouncer, keeping the hooks up and away from snags, but they don't interfere with hooking fish because they usually attach from behind.

Jon Rasmussen
Menasha, Wisconsin

Daddy, Help!

I am not an avid fisherman; however, when the chance is there, I take full benefit to go. Once the opportunity to take my 5-year-old daughter with me arose and we went. A friend from Ft. Bragg, North Carolina took us to a little manmade lake (more like a big pond) that an old man had built, simply asking for a $1 donation when you went, to cover the upkeep of the lake. We weren't having too much luck for a few hours into the day; then my daughter kept saying she could see a fish. She was standing over by a pipe where the lake drained into a little water hole. I really paid no attention, and told her, "Well, throw your line in and catch him." She smiled and did so. About 5 minutes later she started screaming for help and I thought she had hooked her finger or something. To my disbelief, she had a fish on. Her pole, which I might add was a little Mickey Mouse green pole we picked up from WalMart, was bent over and she was losing ground. So I steadied her and held her belt loop while she slowly reeled in. It turned out the little bluegill was an 8-pound largemouth bass. I guess it really ain't a tip as such, but, when you take your child fishing and you hear, "Daddy, I see one," don't blow it off.

James and Taylar Morse
Via E-mail

The Birthday Bass

Have you ever wanted to catch something special for your birthday or a similar occasion? No doubt, some of you have.

Well, one July, just two days before my sixteenth birthday, I had just such a wish. However, this desire was further magnified by the fact that I knew this would be my last chance to fish before I would be required to purchase a fishing license in accordance with state laws, and I wanted to make the most of it.

I decided upon a small private pond in Candia, New Hampshire, which I had fished a great deal that year. It was a prize pond, having been stocked with largemouth bass in the past. Its shallow waters gave way to remarkable bass fishing with such soft baits as the Lunkercity Baby Sluggo and the Yamamoto Senko.

I started out early, hoping to fill my plate with one of these bass for my birthday, and thus begins my tale. I slowly trudged back along the rough trail that followed the pond's edge, in the direction of the roadway where my ride was to arrive in about 15 to 20 minutes. I sighed. Despite the wildlife being as refreshing as usual, I had worn myself out in determination to catch my birthday bass. I had already had a few good bass get off my line, off a small point along the shore. It was my favorite place to cast, with underwater rocks offshore and an abandoned beaver lodge right nearby.

After losing my fish in that area and realizing the bass weren't biting anymore, I had continued to the opposite shore. Still no luck. Discouraged and upset about the losses, I now trudged back along the pine needle trail. I glanced off gloomily toward the point. Suddenly, there was a ripple. Then came the majestic jump of a bass. My heart skipped a beat, but then I sighed again. I couldn't decide whether to pursue the chance. I knew it would be a good chance, but I was running out of time and energy.

When I came to the fork in the path, between going to the road and fishing, I chose the quest out of determination to catch my birthday bass. When I got out onto the point, I first cast to my left, as it was the direction I thought the bass might have been traveling. Two casts. Nothing. I now saw my father emerge from the opening in the path to the road. I cast to the right where it first jumped. Weeds? NO. Something is moving down there and reflecting a golden glow from the sun. I reeled.

Up came a bass! It sprang from the water again, boasting its size. My eyes widened. My hands shook. I kept on reeling. My father was now crashing through the brush toward me as I brought onto shore the largest bass I had ever caught. The bass thrashed and wriggled from time to time in my hands, on the way to my grandparent's, my uncle and aunt's, and finally my home, but I loved every moment of it. The bass weighed 5 pounds, measuring 20 inches in length and was 15 inches in girth.

Though it may not seem large in the South, had I been aware sooner and brought him to a taxidermist, he would have been eligible for the New Hampshire Trophy Fish Program. So, I set out for a birthday meal and ended up with one awesome birthday present (tasted great, too). Furthermore, it's great knowing that it was my last fish of my "fishing childhood" (before I needed an adult license).

It just goes to show that perseverance and determination in fishing pays off. I caught my bass with a brown-crayfish-colored, shallow-diving, Bomber Model A crankbait.

Stephen Bond
Candia, New Hampshire

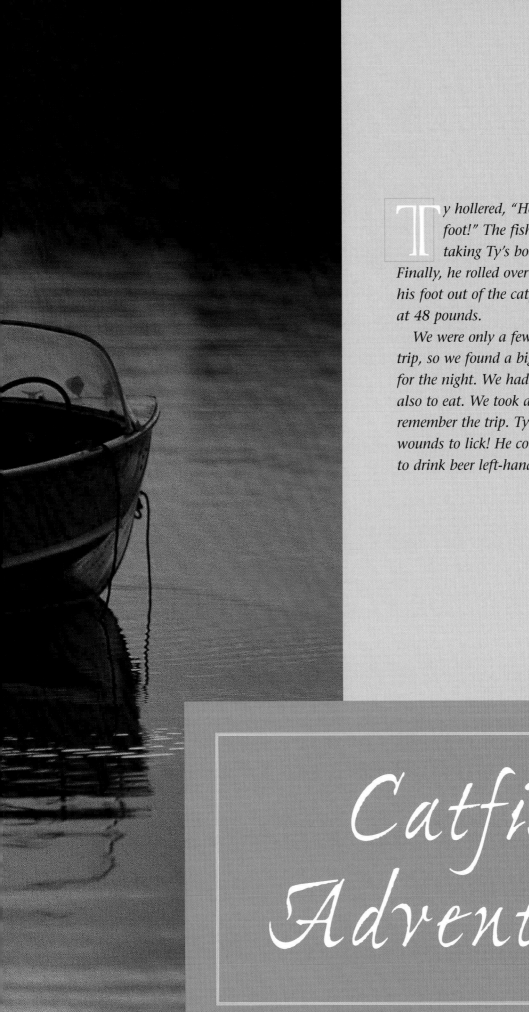

Ty hollered, "Help me get this fish off my foot!" The fish was jumping around and taking Ty's body right along with it. Finally, he rolled over and they were able to get his foot out of the catfish's mouth. It weighed in at 48 pounds.

We were only a few miles from the end of the trip, so we found a big sandbar and camped there for the night. We had a lot of fish to clean and also to eat. We took all kinds of pictures to remember the trip. Tyrone and I also had some wounds to lick! He could hardly walk, and I had to drink beer left-handed for a couple of days.

—From "Hoggin' for Cats"

Catfish Adventures

Hoggin' for Cats

My third wife, Renee, and I moved our portable house, or I suppose I should put it, our 28-foot tag-along trailer, to a little town called Union in Missouri, the "SHOW ME" state. I had just started to work at the Chrysler plant in St. Louis.

After a couple of months of working 6 days a week, 10 hours a day, we finally had 3 days off because of a holiday. I and a few of the other "boomers" I was working with decided to take a float trip down the Meramec River. There were about a dozen Missouri natives we had met at the local tavern who all had 12- to 14-foot aluminum boats. All were experienced at the art of "hoggin'."

For those of you who don't know what hoggin' is, it's simply reaching your arm inside a submerged log, sticking your hand inside a catfish's mouth, and pulling it out! This was explained to me by a friend of mine by the name of Tyrone. He owned the tavern and was also my guide on the trip. He was a tall, lanky man, about 50 years old, and had lived on this river all his life.

The third person in our boat was Tyrone's son, Tim. He was 14 years old and told me he'd been hoggin' for 10 years. "It's a blast!"

If a 14-year-old can do this and has been doing it for years, COOL! Let's hog us a catfish. I was convinced there was nothing to it!

We unloaded our gear. All together there were 8 aluminum boats and 18 people for a 3-day float down the Meramec River.

Tyrone seemed to know every log along the way. We paddled over to one. He said, "This is always a good log." It was stuck in the bank; the log was hollow and just under the surface of the water. A turtle slid off the top of the log. Ty turned to me and said, "You have to be careful not to stick your hand in a turtle's mouth." That's when I realized that snapping turtles and water moccasins also like to hang around old tree logs. As a Florida boy, I wouldn't think of sticking my hand in an alligator's mouth. Why would I want to do this?

Ty slid out of the boat, and Tim and I went alongside of the log. Tyrone stuck his head underwater and reached inside the log. After about 15 seconds he came back up for air and said, "It's a nice fish, but I can't reach her!"

Tim immediately knew what to do. He grabbed the net and got on the bank. There was a knothole on top of the log, and he stuck the handle of the net in the hole. Ever so gently he pushed the fish closer to the front of the log. Ty took a deep breath and went back under. A couple of seconds later, the bubbles began to fly, and up popped Ty holding a 16-pound catfish by the mouth. His hand, past his wrist, was inside the fish's mouth and his fingers were sticking out the fish's gills. The fish was shaking and jumping and ready for a fight, but you could clearly see that Ty had complete control of the fish. Situation in hand, so to speak. He threw the fish in the boat.

We put up $5.00 per boat for bragging rights to the biggest fish, and another $5.00 for the most poundage within the legal limits of the fish. I could see we were on our way to winning both titles.

Soon we headed back down the river and pulled up to another log. Tim slid out of the boat and into the water. He looked at me and said, "I'll show you even a kid can do this." I just sat in the boat and watched as Tim dove under the water, reached inside the log, and pulled out another catfish. This one was 11 pounds. Tim explained with fish in hand, "There's nothing to it!"

I smiled back, and as he tossed the catfish in the boat I said, "I guess not." But this time I had a lump in my throat because I knew I was next!

We had floated about a mile along this peaceful river when we rounded a bend and a big smile came across Ty's face. Not a good sign! Ty hollers up to me, "I've always got a catfish out of this log, Charlie." He was talking to me.

This big log was stuck in a small logjam in the bend of the river. The opening of the log was facing away from the current and was about 3 feet under water. Ty said, "Just remember what you have seen, and JUST DO IT!"

Well, I remembered. I remembered the water moccasins and the snapping turtles. I'm going to stick my hand where? I looked at Tim and thought, "The kid didn't have a problem at all!" I couldn't let this kid embarrass me. They would never let me live it down at work, or at the tavern, if I didn't go. I had to do it!

Well, I was mentally ready for it, but my body didn't want to get into the water. I took a deep breath and slid out of the boat, into the water. It was cold! Maybe there won't be a fish in this log, and we can skip my turn. No dice!

"Go get 'em, Charlie," Ty said. I took a deep breath, stood at the side of the log, went under, and opened my eyes. I looked all around the log at first to check for whatever. Then I looked inside the log. It was dark, but I could see something pull back farther into the darkness of the log. I was out of air! I came to the surface. The log

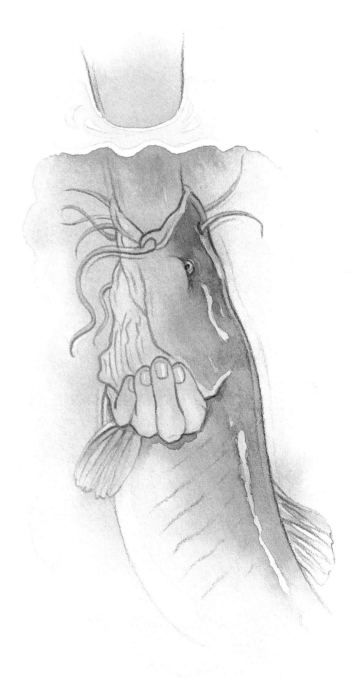

was only 3 feet down, but it seemed a lot farther. I stood up, touched the bottom, and got my footing. I was standing in just under 5 feet of water. It was good to know I could stand up. I told Ty there was a catfish in the log, but I couldn't get a good look at it! He said, "I'll fix that," and got out of the boat with the net. He said, "I'll push it toward you."

I said, "Gulp. OK." I took a couple of deep breaths and went under again. That was the only way I could keep my knees from shaking so bad. I looked inside the log and there it was. A huge catfish, looking directly at me, with all its whiskers going in different directions, slowly opening and closing its mouth to breathe. I reached in the log and touched its face. The fish moved back, and I was out of air again. I surfaced once more, and told Ty it moved back farther in the log.

He said he could feel it move past the handle of the net. He had a series of holes on top of the log, and he could bring the catfish back out to me. I looked over at Tim. He motioned to me to stick my hand down its throat, turn my hand, grab a gill, and pull it out. I nodded and took a couple more deep breaths. Boy, were my knees shaking now! I took one last breath and went under again.

I don't know if it was Ty pushing the fish to the end of the log or my knees shaking so much it sucked the fish to the opening. But there it was! I saw it open its mouth. I did what I was supposed to do, and I shoved my hand deep into the fish's mouth, turned my hand, and grabbed it by the gills. I wasn't ready for what happened next!

The fish pulled back with authority and smashed my head on the top of the log and my body, in the ribs, on the bottom of the log. Well, when that happened I must have lost half the air I had in my lungs. There were bubbles everywhere, and I know they didn't all come out of my mouth! I pulled back.

I knew I was on my own, under water, with a fight for life. My own life! That fish had me pinned to the opening of the log. I felt my feet touch the bank. I thought, "Now I can get some leverage on the fish." Wham! It pulled me back into the log, and it was shaking me like a dog would shake you playing with a towel. My elbow seemed like a limp piece of spaghetti, shaking and pulling me, jammed up against the log.

It's amazing what goes through your mind at a moment like this. This fish could drown me! I got my footing on the bank one more time, with my left arm on the end of the log. My face hurt, my ribs were hurting, and my right arm was in the mouth of a giant in its own habitat.

Florida boy, think 'gator! No, it was just a catfish! I gave a mighty pull with all that my body could muster. The fish came out. I thought, "Yeah!" Then it went to the bottom of the river. I thought, "Wrong way!" I

pushed up from the bottom with fish in hand. Tyrone was standing there, with the working end of the fish net coming right up alongside me, netting the catfish and my arm. Problem is, I have to let go of the catfish, and he still thinks he has me! The way he's shaking me, I'm beginning to think he does have me! Looking at my arm, I would say, "That noodle's done!"

Tyrone hollered, "Let go! Let go!" I looked at him. He had the net in his hand and was motioning me to let go. I opened my fist, and I could feel the fish slip right off my arm—a feeling I will never forget. Tyrone had the fish in the net. I got under the fish, and we put her inside the boat. I was standing there, just numb, looking at the catfish inside the boat. Cheers went up from a few of the boats in the area, and Tim said, "Good job, Charlie."

I reached to shake his hand and noticed, from my elbow down to my hand, I was scratched and bleeding. But I don't think I broke anything! Tyrone, who was in the water now, reached over to me, slipped, and gave me a head butt. We both stopped in our tracks, hands on our heads, and started laughing. I noticed I had a bruise over my right eye where the catfish slammed me into the log. I was bruised in the ribs, too, but I had the first catfish of my life without a rod and reel. The catfish weighed in at 26 pounds!

We made camp a couple of miles down the river. We had a feast, and fried up both catfish and smallmouth bass, potatoes and onions, with corn on the cob. It was a nice night. Most of us just lay around the campfire telling stories. When dawn came we started floating down the river again when Ty said, "I got a good log up ahead. I'll do this one."

We rounded another bend in the river and paddled the boat into position alongside the log. It was just another old logjam, the way I looked at it. Not to Ty! He slipped into the water and walked slowly over to the log. I thought he was going to work on the log you could see about 2 feet under water. Not a chance! He explained it to me. "There's another log 4 feet down. It must be a redwood because it's so big around you can swim into it. That's where the big one is at!"

I thought to myself, "You're right! This one's for you!"

It was about 7 feet in the deepest part of the river. "But," Tyrone said, "I'm 6 feet, 3 inches. I can bounce the rest of the way up." He took a breath and submerged, took a look in the log, and came back up about 15 seconds later. He told me to grab the net and get on top of the log to help push out the fish. He said it was a big catfish down there, and he didn't think he could put his hand in its mouth. He would have to use his foot!

I said, "What?"

He said, "Yeah. All I have to do is put my foot into its mouth, turn sideways, and pull the fish out!"

I got out of the boat thinking about what he had said. "Put my foot into its mouth and turn sideways." I almost slipped off the log just thinking about it. Luckily I had the net in my hand and was able to catch myself.

Ty said, "Quiet! You'll scare the fish." I put the handle of the net in the knothole real easy. Tim was in our boat near the front of the log, and the three other boats sort of formed a circle around the front of the log in the middle of the river. Ty gave us a thumbs-up sign, took a

deep breath and went under.

I could feel the fish back up with the handle of the net, so I tried to nudge it to the front. I probably had the best seat in the house. I could see Ty looking into the hole, then he pushed away and stuck his leg in the log. I could see him all of a sudden jam his foot and turn sideways. Then the water just seemed to explode. With his other leg on the log he pushed away and pulled the fish out. Immediately the fish headed down.

It was big enough to take Ty down with it. You know it; they were in the deepest part of the river. I saw Ty turn his knee upward and grab the fish. With his other leg he pushed off the bottom. He came out of the water, TAIL FIRST. Fish tail first, that is. He had the fish thrown across his chest, with the tail of the fish well over his head. He had a good grip on the fish, with his foot still in the catfish's mouth.

He hollered to the guys in the boat. "Pull me in the boat!" He went down again under water. A couple of seconds later he shot back up. Two of the guys grabbed him by the hair of his head, then grabbed him by the arms, and pulled him into the boat. The boat rocked and almost tipped over. The people in the other boats kept the catch boat upright. There they were, grown men sprawled out in the boat and one of them with a catfish dangling off his leg.

Ty hollered, "Help me get this fish off my foot!" The fish was jumping around and taking Ty's body right along with it. Finally, he rolled over and they were able to get his foot out of the catfish's mouth. It weighed in at 48 pounds.

We were only a few miles from the end of the trip, so we found a big sandbar and camped there for the night. We had a lot of fish to clean and also to eat. We took all kinds of pictures to remember the trip. Tyrone and I also had some wounds to lick! He could hardly walk, and I had to drink beer left-handed for a couple of days.

Charles P. Wilson
Olympia, Washington

Reunion on the River

It was a hot summer afternoon and I was at my favorite fishing hole below a dam on the Rock River with about 20 other people. Most of them were fishing for flathead or walleye. I was tossing a leadhead with a white twister tail, having little luck. I had been fishing about 4 hours and landed a few small walleye and sauger and a couple of gar. Over all, not much success.

Halfway across the dam I spotted someone who was fighting something very big. I watched him fight it for about 15 minutes, and finally he landed what I would say to be about a 20-pound flathead. I made my way over to him to take a look. I began to talk to the fisherman, and I thought to myself, I know this guy.

We went to high school together. We didn't really know each other that well, as we had nothing in common. He was into hot rods and I was into sports. The crowds didn't get along very well.

We fished next to each other for the rest of the day and I didn't catch a thing, but it was still one of the most exciting days of fishing I've had. We were both using the same jig and the same color twister tail and throwing at the same tree that had gone halfway over the waterfall. Over the next couple of hours, my newfound fishing buddy had caught a couple of nice-size walleye and two more big flatheads, all of which he landed with the help of my net. I guess I will take the assist on those catches.

By this time I was getting pretty discouraged. How come he gets the fish when we throw at the same place with the same jig and color? Next thing you know, he hooks onto the mother lode. At this time I'm guessing it's another flathead. He continues to fight it for about a half hour. In the meantime, everybody who was wading has come over to see what he has on the other end of his line. All of a sudden there is no more fight. The large fish had gone under the tree and wrapped up around a limb. After trying to pull it free for a while, he decided to cut the line. I looked at him and said, "ARE YOU CRAZY? Give him some slack; maybe he will free himself from the tree."

You could see the fish pulling a little, but he was tangled up pretty good. I told my buddy that I would go up and see if I could unhook the fish from the tree. I walked up to the tree and as I got closer the water got deeper and swifter.

By this time it was about 4 to 5 feet deep and very difficult to keep from getting swept back downstream. I finally reached the tree and began to dive down and feel around to see if I could release the line. Keep in mind, when my feet left the river bottom to dive down it was like running on a treadmill. Swim like hell and get nowhere fast.

It took about a dozen attempts, but I finally got to the fish and untangled the line and came up with a huge flathead. Everybody around started yelling and cheering. With my hand in the huge mouth of the fish I picked my feet up off the river bottom and floated back to my buddy and gave him his fish. He then put it on the stringer and gave me a high five.

I looked at the stringer and asked him, "That is a lot of fish, what are you going to do with them?" His reply was, "Let them go." I told him to wait and I would go get someone from the bait shop to weigh them and take his picture. While I was gone he caught one more for a total of 5 flatheads weighing well over 100 pounds. We let the fish go, had a couple of beers, talked and laughed about the best fishing day either of us had had.

I went back every weekend for the rest of the summer and ran into my buddy a couple more times, and we still talk about that great Saturday afternoon of fishing. I don't live in the area anymore, but my folks do, and anytime I go visit them I take my dogs out there to run around, hoping to see him again. I haven't run into him since that summer, but I think about that day and the great fun we had. It's a shame it took so long to get to know him, and hopefully our paths will cross again. Thanks, Sean, for the great memories and hope to see you at the fishing hole again soon.

Keith Stegemann
Rockford, Illinois

Man Versus Cat

When I received the call from my buddy, Jeff Laures, inviting me to go fishing at our "honey hole" the following morning, I answered with, "Yes—let's go", on the condition that we rendezvous at 11 a.m. rather than the suggested 6 a.m. meeting time. Hey, a man needs his sleep!

Picking up Jeff and his three boys went well as we left Dallas and headed north. Jeff's boys, Brandon, 3½, Benjamin, 5½ and Zachary, 5½ (twins) were full of anticipation as the "big bass" stories were told and retold. All of us had fished this spot many times, and many big bass were caught and released. Little did we know that today was going to be different than most.

We pulled the Suburban up to the bank and we proceeded to start catching bluegill, which we used to catch the bass. After 30 minutes, we had caught a few bass in the 3- to 5-pound range, but the little boys were getting impatient and wanted bigger fish! They came running up to me and asked, "Chuck, what do we need to do to catch a bigger fish?" After some thought, I answered with, "We need to change the music in the tape player in the Suburban; that should do it!" So I marched over to the vehicle and changed the tape. Who ever said fishermen were superstitious!

I walked over and picked up my 8½-foot heavy-action Loomis rod outfitted with a Shimano Chronarch reel with 12-pound Triple Fish line. Reaching into our bucket, I picked out a bluegill that was about average size and placed him on my big treble hook, then made a nice long cast from the bank. The bluegill hit the water and proceeded to swim down and out of sight.

All of a sudden the line flew off the reel with tremendous speed and power. Knowing the underwater structure like the back of my hand, I knew I had to stop this fish ASAP, because two huge underwater trees loomed in the pathway of that line.

I immediately engaged the reel and set the hook. The pole and reel nearly jumped out of my hands due to the power. At this point, the line was ready to break because of the tension, so I ran with the pole toward the bank to release the pressure on the line. I couldn't believe the power I was feeling and was praying that the line wouldn't break. I was pushing the pole out as far as I could toward the runaway fish. Things were happening so fast I couldn't adjust the drag. I hit the free spool once again and let her rip. The line continued to rip off the reel at a tremendous speed and all I could do was watch.

Looking down at the spool I noticed there was only about 50 feet of line left. I engaged the reel once more and set the hook again. I set the hook a second time, which slowed the fish down, and finally the fish actually stopped its forward movement.

The fish then pulled me down (the pole); then I pulled it back ever so gently. Jeff came running over and asked what was happening. I replied that if this was a bass, it would probably be the Texas State Record! Jeff, of course, gave me a doubting look and said something to the effect that it was probably "a little fish."

It was apparent that the fish was going nowhere and actually appeared stuck. I attempted various angles to try and free the fish, with no luck. Then I remembered a very unpleasant experience I had fishing Spring Lake in northern California. You know, the lake where my good friend, Paul Duclos, caught the 24-pound bass. Back in November of the previous year I had a 20-pound-class bass on my line that wrapped up in my anchor rope. When I pulled the rope up, it broke the line and the big bass swam away. The flashbacks of that moment hit me like a ton of bricks and I wasn't going to let that happen again. At that moment, I handed Jeff the pole and told him to hold it—I was going in after the fish!

Jeff looked at me with one of the funniest expressions I had ever seen, and he exclaimed, "YOU'RE WHAT?" I said, "I'm going in; I'm not about to lose that huge fish!" So off with my clothes, right down to my boxer shorts, and I grabbed the line and waded into the water.

I started to swim, holding the 12-pound-test line ever so gently, and began to weave around some of the submerged trees that I knew were present. I swam out about 20 feet, when my knee hit one of the trees, and pain set in. I knew nothing was broken, but it sure did hurt.

Continuing on, I swam out about 75 feet from the shore to where I was right over the fish. As I treaded water, I could feel the fish pulling the line. I knew at this point I was right on top of him. So with a big breath of air, I dove down toward whatever awaited me. Reaching a depth of what I estimated to be about 10 feet, I could see about 4 to 5 feet in front of me. I then saw a patch of hydrilla and, by the feel of the line, the fish seemed to be right in front of me; probably wrapped up in the hydrilla. I ran out of air, surfaced for more, then plunged right back down. This time, I saw the fish! It was GIGANTIC and dark, and I estimated it at 4 feet long—in fact, it appeared to be so big, it scared me! I swam back up for more air and yelled to Jeff that the fish was not a bass, but a HUGE catfish! Holding the line and shaking in my undershorts, I dove back down and actually moved the fish out and away from the hydrilla—MISTAKE! This freed up line and now the big cat was on the move again–with me hanging on! I spooled the line because I was out of breath and had to surface while the cat was once again trying to get away. Once I reached the top, I grabbed the line again and the cat actually pulled me through the water for about 10 feet before stopping. The line was taut and the cat wasn't going anywhere.

As I swam over to the big fish, it was an amazing sight to see that fish on the top of the water. I gently reached one arm over the top of it and slid my left hand into its mouth in an attempt to get hold of it; this, while trying to stay afloat. After I got my hand it its mouth, the big cat clamped down on my hand and I could now feel more pain. The teeth and the roof of his mouth must have cut my hand. I felt that I had secured the fish and when I tried to move with it, I couldn't budge it because the line from my pole that Jeff was holding was taut.

The fish wanted to move away from the shore. I wanted to move him back toward the shore, but he didn't want anything to do with it. I yelled back to Jeff to cut the line at the pole to release the tension. That made all the difference in the world. I now turned the head of the big cat and started back toward the shore, about 75 feet away. I was amazed because the fish was just as tired as I was. It wasn't fighting, just going along for the ride. I was very careful as I approached the shore not to hit those submerged trees again and as I looked up, Jeff was taking pictures of me hauling this big cat back.

Exhaustion was overtaking me, and about 5 feet away from Jeff's outstretched arms and the shore, I lost hold of the fish. The big cat started to sink, and then he was moving away from me! Panic and adrenaline took over and I mustered what strength I had left, dove under the water, and grabbed the fish once again. I kicked over to Jeff and pushed the big fish up to Jeff's arms. His hand caught the hook when he grabbed the mouth of the fish and he let out a scream. I immediately rolled over on my back and just sat there in the water trying to get my strength. Jeff's boys were all yelling at the sight of this monster fish, nicknaming it "Shark" and "Goliath."

Pulling myself out of the water and feeling a little

like Tarzan, I walked over to the Suburban and grabbed my big fish tank from the back of the vehicle. It's a large Rubbermaid storage bin that I use to hold the fish while I get ready to take pictures, measurements, etc. We filled the bin with water and placed the big cat into it. The only challenge was the cat didn't fit lengthwise. So we had to carefully turn the tail of the gigantic fish to make it fit.

I grabbed my scale, measuring tape and camera, and we prepared to document the fish. We waited a few minutes so the cat could stabilize. The cat appeared to be adapting well to his little tank and we started the measurements. We first weighed the fish, and my electronic scale jumped to 35.8 pounds, then settled at 33 pounds! Not bad for 12-pound test! Next, the tape I had only went to 36 inches. After cutting and saving the first 3 feet from the hook, we cut the line to the exact length of the fish. Our measurements determined the big cat to be 45 inches long! Next, we cut line around the exact girth of the cat, which measured out at 23½ inches. We ended up with exact measurements, and saved the line cuts for length, girth and the 3 feet of line to the hook.

After awhile, I started to feel compassion for the fish. Being held and photographed and listening to all the hooting and hollering from the little kids, including the two big little boys, was probably more attention than this big fish had had since he was born. But the best was yet to come …

Releasing the fish gave me incredible feelings, knowing that this fish was going to live. Sure, we could have fed 50 people over a barbecue or had the fish mounted, but to see that cat swim off was a moment in my life that I'll never forget.

More deep feelings and emotions were experienced with the phone call I received later that night. While at home, nursing that very sore hand the cat had clamped its jaw on earlier in the day, I received a phone call from Shonda Laures, the mother of Brandon, Benjamin, and Zachary. Shonda shared the excitement of her boys with me and retold the story in their words! Better yet, she thanked me for the gift I gave those boys as they watched catch-and-release in its true form, something they'll never forget and something I'm sure they will pass along as well. Mother Nature, very happy and pleased with what we'd experienced, smiled down upon five little boys that day!

Jerry Bull Baylor
Leechburg, Pennsylvania

Recipe Poetry

Ya want to catch some catfish,
This is what you do.
Pick up your rod and reel and
Grab some bait too.
Head to your favorite stream or pond
And find yourself a hole.
Get out your bait and then rig up
Your pole.
Cast out your line and give a
Little wait.
Catch a few catfish while using up
Your bait.
Pick up your catfish and clean 'em
The way you do.
Get out this recipe, it will tell
You what to do.
Take 'em fillets of catfish and lay
'Em on some foil.
Treat 'em very gently like your
Favorite girl.
This recipe is easy and can be made very quick.
Now use enough butter so your
Fish won't stick.
Put butter and lemon pepper on
Foil with your fish.
Wrap it up snugly, you will soon
Have your wish.
Lay this on a grill or on top of
Some hot coals.
Get in your pack and you can butter
Up the rolls.
By the time that little job is over,
You should smell the fish.
Roll the foil packages over, now go
Get your dish.
Now that that job is done, you
Are ready to eat.
Now don't you agree that this
Is a very easy treat?

—Jerry Bull Baylor
Leechburg, Pennsylvania

The Big One

It was a cool November evening around 5:00 p.m. It was the perfect evening for fishing. Little did I know how strange it would turn out.

My friend Steven and I were at our apartment complex's canal. I grew up fishing in Wisconsin on lakes, so even though I've lived in Florida for years, fishing canals was a relatively new experience. Especially since I didn't have a regular Florida fishing buddy until Steven came along.

We weren't getting too many bites, so we baited our hooks for what would be the last cast of the night. As I slipped a chunk of Colby-Jack cheese onto my hook, I hoped for the big one to hit, though I was quite skeptical. We dropped our lines off of a concrete slab. Below us, there was a submerged bike rack. There was also a little corner where the bank of a jutting-out piece of land met the slab where we were standing. In that corner there was about 8 feet of water. Steven and I had dropped our lines about 4 feet apart in that little area.

We waited awhile and finally the big hit came! It hit BOTH of our lines at about the same time. We both pulled up sharply to set the hook. My hook was the one that was set firmly. I was in for a fight that made the wait worthwhile! My pole was a really small one with 6-pound-test line. As I played the fish and reeled it in, my rod bent, and I could feel the strength of this fish. Finally, I could see the white, fat, speckled belly at the surface of the murky water. I had absolutely NO idea what species of fish this was. I was saying to myself how it was too fat to be a bass and that trout don't live in canals. Steven grabbed my pole and pulled it out of the water. It was the one type of fish I never wanted to catch. A catfish.

Now, this was about 2 years ago, so I was a little more frightened than I would be now. I figured Steven, being a typical boy, would chase me with it, so I ran. When I came back all he asked was, "Can I show my dad?" He dragged the channel cat all the way to our hallway. My brother had run ahead and told my mom and grandma about the fish. Sure enough, there they were, waiting with the camera! As we all observed, Steven's mom came out with a towel and took the fish in it and unhooked it. Then, she put it in a spaghetti pot full of water. The fish was 15 inches long and weighed 4 pounds. This was the first good look at it I'd gotten. We carried the pot to the canal. Steven's dad came along and threw it back. It landed in the water with a satisfying SPLASH that ended that wonderful day.

• My tip to all my fellow fishing fanatics is the only one that will never fail. Be patient, and "the big one" will come to you!

Brenna Dixon
Coral Springs, Florida

Midnight Catfish

In the summer of 1999, my cousins Danielle, Courtney, Ashley, and Gordon and I went to the Norwalk Reservoir for a midnight fishing trip for catfish. I caught two catfish, each 14 inches long. My cousins caught two 13-inch cats. We used chicken liver for bait. The water was murky, with about 1-foot waves. With 7-foot rods and baitcasting reels, we had no trouble getting them in to shore. We got home around 3:30 a.m. By 9:00 a.m. we had them filleted and, boy, were they good!

Derrick Brown
Shiloh, Ohio

Thanks, Grandma

Hi, my name is Jeremy Henley, I live in Poplar Creek, Mississippi. It is a small rural area, population of about 250 to 300. I would like to share a story about someone dear to me who greatly influenced my love of fishin'.

I called her Grandma Gladys—she was my great-grandmother on my father's side. I was probably 4 or 5. Grandma loved cat fishin'. She had become too aged to fish the river, so my granddaddy, Clayton (her son), would catch some good flatheads, bluecats or channels from the Big Black River and put them in the small pond behind Grandma's house.

I visited Grandma on a daily basis, for we only lived about a mile or so apart. As I remember, she had one rod and reel and several good canes. Grandma had her own fishing attire, too. She'd put on that old kitchen apron, her straw hat and, as always, go barefooted with her pants rolled up to her shins.

We would walk down through the pasture down by the barn and find us some nightcrawlers or grub worms and to the pond we would go. Grandma had an old wood chair that she'd sit on, and I'd stand alongside. We mostly used the cane poles.

I remember one day in particular that I'll never forget. Grandma and me started in a-catchin' perch and for a little feller I was having a ball. Now, Grandma had an old tom cat that liked to go with us, and thinkin' back now I don't blame him. We were probably there half the day catchin' perch and the old cat would get a few. That day we caught 65 perch and that memory has been with me ever since.

Now, I have had some good fishin' trips since, and bigger and far more glamorous, but the times I spent with Grandma on the bank of that small pond shine far brighter to me.

Now I have children of my own—two boys, a 2-year-old and a 4-year-old. I purchased Grandma's place after her and Granddaddy passed away. I started my oldest son fishin' last spring in the same little pond, and hope the youngest can get goin' this year.

• I don't really have a fishin' tip per se, but I do know that time spent fishin' with a youngster can shape their interest toward constructive things and wonderful memories. So all said, I owe a big thanks to Grandma for the lessons, the fishin' and the wonderful memories.

Jeremy Henley
Kilmichael, Mississippi

No More Mess

We all get worm dirt all over boat carpet. Here is what I do to stop this mess. I lay a large bath towel on the floor, then put the worm container on the towel. So, when you pull out the worms, the dirt lands on the towel, not the boat. When done, just shake the dirt over the side. This works great when fishing with messy friends.

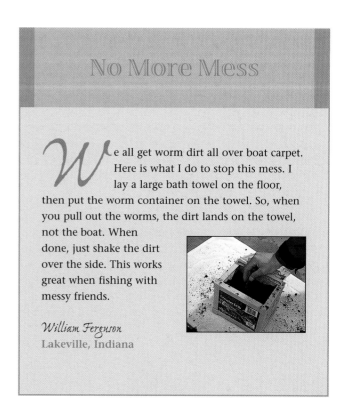

William Ferguson
Lakeville, Indiana

Chicken for Cats

My tip on catching catfish is to use chicken liver tied up in nylon stockings, and to use a line with more than one hook on it at a time. You use 3 or 4 hooks on one line, 8 to 12 inches apart, with a hook at the bottom, then a weight, then the rest of the hooks, 8 to 12 inches apart. I taught my friend to fish this way, the same way an old man taught me when I was a boy.

Wayne Evans
Tampa, Florida

Editor's Note:
Be sure to check state and local regulations on multiple hook usage.

Rod Proposition

When a rod and reel is propped up in a Y-shaped stick, wind and current often make it difficult to keep the line taut enough to detect a bite from movement of the rod tip. Hang a plastic bobber on the line between the bottom two ferrules of the rod. Any movement of the hook will result in an obvious movement of the bobber.

John R. Campbell
Cascade,
Maryland

Great Carp Baits

Here are some unusual, but effective, carp baits I learned from Frank Conrad, a legendary piscator from central Pennsylvania.

1. Mix dry oatmeal and dry Jello mix in a recloseable plastic bag. Place some of the dry mix in your palm, add a few drops of water, roll into a ball and apply to hook.

2. Use a small pin drill to bore holes for your hook in Purina Dog Chow or Gravy Train dry dog food. The flavor blends in the water and attracts the fish.

3. Poor Man's Salmon Eggs work as well as the real things. To make them, add red food coloring to canned corn. For flavor, add either vanilla extract or fish oil.

John R. Campbell
Cascade, Maryland

There in my favorite of all fishing places, I held the small rainbow in my hands, and brought it close to Conlyn. I wanted him to see its deep reds and blues. He was reaching as I was moving toward him. The trout flipped from my hands and was gone before he could touch the wet skin. I took Conlyn's hand and moved toward home, hoping that, someday, he will repeat the journey over and over—there beside me.

—From "There Beside Me"

Chasing
Trout & Salmon

When in Doubt, Kick 'Em Out

We don't get to go fishing often, so when we go to Spencer Pond for a precious week, we like to take advantage of every minute we have and fish like crazy.

This particular visit, we were having an especially hard time catching fish. Everything was different—the weather, the water conditions, even the expectations of the other people at the camps. Fly fishing was "in" and worms were passé. We'd never catch anything with worms, we were told. To top it off, the day was blustery and the pond choppy, with whitecaps. Not very good conditions for going out in a canoe.

Desperate to get our lines wet, we fished from the floating dock near the shore. The dock is a large square platform made of strips of wood with spaces between them easily big enough for a good-sized fish to escape through. A narrower walkway of the same construction attaches the dock to the shore. The water between the dock and the shore is about knee deep or in a little shallower. Shiners, chubs and yellow perch are the predominant fish around the shore, though there are nice trout other places in the pond, so we didn't expect to catch anything else. Still, a nice mess of fried perch makes a tasty dinner, and we were looking forward to it.

All of a sudden, my fishing buddy hooks what is unmistakably a trout—and a good-sized one, too (and on one of those worms that would never catch anything). After reeling it in, she heads for the shore so that the fish can't escape through the gaps in the dock. As she crosses the walkway, the trout, which has been wriggling on the line she's holding, gives an almighty heave and flips off the hook into the water between the dock and the shore.

Without a moment's hesitation, my partner jumps into the water after it, shouting, "I've worked too hard for you to get away now." She kicks, connects, and the fish sails onto the shore. I'm useless, as I've collapsed with laughter on the end of the dock. It's a beautiful fish.

In a delicious irony, the fly fishermen congregate. "What are you using for bait?" they cry. "Worms." In great astonishment, they admire the fish. Nine inches. Delicious. And here's my tip:

• Use all the resources you have to land your fish!

Deborah L. Scheetz
Dracut, Massachusetts

Investing in the Future

This happened about 12 years ago on the first day of trout fishing season near my home: This particular stream is best fished with success using maggots or mealworms. While fishing, I happened to see two young boys, who had just arrived, begin fishing below me. What caught my eye was the heavy equipment and the large spinners they were using. They were ready for bass, not trout.

I reeled in and walked down stream to where the boys were fishing. We spoke and asked the usual question, "Having any luck?" They told me they hadn't had a bite yet. I asked if I could offer some help and advice? Each boy's line was too heavy (10 to 12 pounds) and lay coiled across the surface of the water. The line had been on their reels for some time. I told them they needed to use lighter line (4-pound test) and when they could, to ask their parents to get them a lighter rod.

They only had the large spinners for bait so I asked if I could help them and maybe make their day on the water a little more pleasant. I had an extra little container and gave them some maggots and mealworms. I gave them some hooks and some split shots. I reeled off some line from my reel and tied it on the end of their line. I told them that was the best I could do to help them. They thanked me and I wished them good luck and I moved downstream.

Later that day I was leaving the stream, heading to my truck, and came upon the same two boys. When they saw me they couldn't wait to show the trout they had caught. They thanked me again. I was very happy for them.

I never saw them again, but I sure hope the little bit of time and effort spent with them encouraged them to continue what I consider the greatest sport in the world—fishing.

David McClain
Sarver, Pennsylvania

Homemade De-Hooker

The cheapest and best de-hooker I have ever used can be made out of an old worn-out toothbrush. An old Japanese fishing friend of mine showed me how to make one.

The hole on the end of some toothbrushes may have to be enlarged with a sharp knife, electric bit or round file, and some of the newer toothbrushes don't have a hole, but can be drilled.

Next, using a hacksaw, cut a slit on one side, as shown:

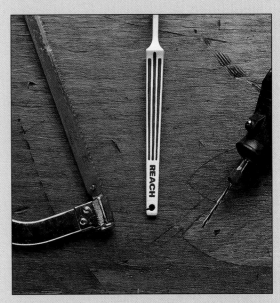

If a fish swallows the hook, slip the line through the slit, keeping the line tight, and push and turn the toothbrush to remove the hook. Works good on tiny trebles too! After dressing the fish, I use the brush to remove the blood along the backbone, so the tool serves two purposes!

Roy Abo
Paul, Idaho

I Told You So!

Every year for the past 12 years I have driven from New Jersey and religiously fished the Salmon River for steelhead and browns with the occasional laker or even a leftover salmon. It was my vacation getaway from the wife and kiddies which I looked forward to with a passion, counting the days. Nothing could stop me. Even with no money it was somehow accomplished without doing without. The wife despised fishing and my daughter was too young to hold a rod (I tried). My son was my faithful apprentice when it came to fishing especially, but he was young and I wasn't ready to take the chance of his lasting dedication. To avoid actually saying no, I

just happened to mention a few stories about the bears along the river along with other little tits and tats.

We all have a fishing buddy. One who is like a second wife that we can dedicate ourselves to faithfully whenever we can get away to fish. Mine was Dave. We didn't really talk or hang out all that much as plain old friends, but when you answered the phone and heard the other one's voice you knew it was fishing time. Every adventure was incomparable to any others. Even skunked we had the best of times. When it came to fishing, as long as we had each other we had no worries.

One year one of my worst fears was realized when my friend informed me he had to move to Florida. That was about 6 years ago. Since then I have unsuccessfully attempted to find a suitable substitute for a fishing partner. What I needed was somebody who would fish from dawn to dusk and never want to leave the water until nature left no alternative. Many a friend proved to be just another want-to-be who got cold, tired or bored, asking, "Are we done yet?" or "Can we go get a beer?"

At one point, I came to the realization that I would have to go alone, and I did so for a couple of years. At least I knew I was gonna fish and that was the bottom line. I called Dave regularly to check in on his new fishing ventures and brag about the Salmon River trips he'd missed. He still says he's gonna make it up for one, every time, but he hasn't yet. The next year I packed everyone up and took the family with me.

I geared up my son, who was 9, and asked the guy whose cabin I stay in to help my son along on the water. This way I figured I could fish while he untangled my son's line. On the third and last day of that year's trip I fished my "secret pool." I had caught my first and biggest steelhead there and mounted it on my living room wall. I always fished it last and it always produced. Standing at the end of the drift coming off a small island in the center of a sharp turn on the river, I sent my son upstream a bit out of the way. He was fishing a fast-moving undercut full of snags. I kept warning him to move to open water, but he insisted he'd stay.

As fate would have it, I had a fish on. It was darting around the river like mad, but never showed itself. My son came with the net, but when we got it in all I had was a 10-incher. We laughed together and he asked to release it. As he did, I asked, "At least we got a fish, right?" His reply to me was one that will haunt me for years. He let the fish go and looking up at me, making full eye contact and in a most confident voice, sincerely said, "That wasn't a fish, Dad. The fish I'm gonna catch is gonna eat yours."

There was a period of silence as we fished with no action. The weather was turning and the wind was picking up. I was trying to hold out on suggesting we pack up and head home. We had a long trip and still had to get the girls. As I began to turn to look upstream at my son to end our adventure I heard a sound. That wonderfully terrific sound. The very one we crave when we've got Steelie Fever. Sure enough, there he was. In my hip waders rolled up at his crotch, in a champion's pose, knees bent, feet securely planted with his arms firmly in control of a 10-foot rod bent like a horseshoe to the water as the drag screamed and the silvery beast danced on its tail along the top of the water.

It took some effort, but he landed her. Wouldn't let me touch it, either. She was a beauty, too. Thirty-three and three quarters of an inch. Two quarters of an inch longer than the one I have on the wall.

An older gentleman fishing upstream had ventured over to witness the event. He walked up to my son and touched his shoulder and said, "You should be proud of yourself, Sonny, grown men spend years trying to get a fish like that and never land them."

When you leave the river at this spot there is a hill about a hundred feet almost straight up. I offered to carry the fish for him and he told me, "No way, Dad—somebody might see you and think it's yours." And when we got back, I said we'd go get it filleted for the trip home.

You know what he said? He said, "No way, you're gonna mount this baby so I can hang it next to yours!" So it was.

I'll never live down the events of that fateful day and the story my son stops to tell anyone that will listen. He always ends his story with, "I told you so!"

Bob Hendricksen Jr.
Linden, New Jersey

Basics and Secrets

The first time I tried to catch a trout, I was about 10 years old. I thought the biggest and newest fishing gear was always the way to go. So I bought a fishing vest, a new wooden net, an expensive fly rod, more rooster tails and flies than you could shake a stick at. I spent every lick of my birthday money on all of this new tackle.

So then, on the opening day I took my small fortune of tackle and went down to The Rocky Broad River in Chimney Rock, North Carolina. As soon as I reared back and flung my fly line into the river, I happened to look up and there was this older man with no vest and no fly rod. He sat down on a rock across the river and started to fish with an old beat-up Zebco 33. I thought to myself that he couldn't catch a cold with that old beat-up rod!

So I kept on fishing and he did, too. At the end of the day, I had only caught three fish, and he had caught his limit. He was about to leave. I stopped him and asked him how in the world did he catch all of those fish with that rod and only 1 rooster tail? He said he had been fishing that river for 30 years, and he knew just where the fish were. He said he used a little secret his dad taught him and it has never once failed to produce fish.

Naturally, I asked him his secret. To my great surprise, he told me! His secret was to pour juice off a couple of cans of whole kernel corn, then pour it into a drink bottle. "When I get to my fishing spot," he said, "I take it out and dip my rooster tail in it before every cast." He said that I would be catching my limit just like he was.

So I tried this, and the next day I caught my limit. That man taught me more about fishing than anyone, because I learned that all that fancy tackle is pretty and nice, but you can be a good fisherman without spending a load of money. I hope this tip will help you as much as it did me!

Daniel Sherman
Shelby, North Carolina

The Firecracker

At 6 a.m. the mist was still rising from the lake. By the time I checked into the "fly-fishing-only" section of Long Island's beautiful Connetquot State Park, the sun was up and warming, and the blue sky showed nary a cloud in sight. It looked like it would be a perfect day for fishing.

I paid my park fee, and ambled over to my reserved "beat" on the lake. I looked down over the small bridge that rose over the spillway, and wasn't surprised to see swarms of large trout holding near the spillway mouth, waiting for food morsels to drift by. I had fished this lake site once before when I had arrived too late to get a wading site on the stream. The trout here were huge, finicky and hard to fool, but I had limited out that time, with a 16- and 17-incher, and was anxious to succeed again.

Because there are so many fly fishers waiting to fish these heavily stocked waters, each person is assigned a fishing site or "beat" for 4 hours. My 4 hours would be over at 11 a.m., so I rigged up quickly and tied on my first fly. I could see trout rising about, so I waited for a few minutes to time the rises, and cast to one. My patience was rewarded with a take. But woe and dismay, he broke off. Either I was too slow on the hookset, or else he might have just spit the hook out. The result was the same either way—no fish. The next hour and a half saw this pattern repeated several more times. I just couldn't get 'em to take the hook.

Somewhere around hour 3, it started warming up, so I took a break and peeled off a few layers of clothing. The day was still beautiful, the weather still perfect, but my luck hadn't improved any, and I was feeling pretty glum.

Just then, a man walked by and said, "Good morning," and we started talking. He told me that just the day before, at around the same time of morning, two Russian guys were knocking 'em dead right here, on the same beat, with a number 20 black midge. I thanked him as he walked off, excited at this new secret knowledge. With less than an hour left, I tied on the closest thing I had to a number 20 black midge, and settled in for the battle.

After 15 minutes had passed, the only thing I was battling was my frustration. Three-and-a-half hours had passed—only a half hour left to fish. And fish all over the place! The water was lousy with them. Some were well over 25 inches, maybe even 30. Desperate, I tied on a #4 weighted green caterpillar, and just let it fall straight down below me. Suddenly, the blood rushed through me with a surge of adrenaline, as a h-u-g-e brown trout (I had thought it a log) quickly moved in on the fly. This was it. This baby was coming home with me. Hey, Hon, grease up the pan and get out the cornmeal. Here we go.

I saw it all as if it were in slow motion. The trout moseyed right up to that baby boy and … swam away. My reaction was to stamp my feet, gnash my teeth, punch the air and let out a string of expletives that cannot be printed here. (Luckily, nobody was within earshot.) With only 15 minutes left to fish, I resigned myself to my fate, and looked one last time in my fly box.

Over the last 3¾ hours, I had tried all the old standbys: dry fly patterns, nymphs of all sizes and colors, scuds, streamers and dragonflies. I had "matched the hatch," tying on several mayfly imitations to approximate the size, shape and color of the ubiquitous insect. I had tied on attractor patterns. Emergers and spinners. Nothing had worked.

Then something in the box caught my eye. During a frivolous mood at my tying bench, I had "invented" a fly of my own design using multi-colored metallic-looking thread that I had bought at a craft store that had gone out of business. In shape and form it resembled a nymph. But, the colorful, reflective, red and blue "twist" thread made it look like a gaudy, textured bauble. For some reason, it reminded me of Independence Day, so I called it a "firecracker." With nothing left to lose, I tied it on and half-heartedly tossed it into the water below me. What happened next was astonishing.

The fly hit the water with barely a splash. As it sunk, I could see it sparkle and glitter, as the sunlight glinted like sparks off its reflective surface. Before it had time to sink even 1 foot, with a gasp, my heart leaped into my throat. Fully 8 to 10 large trout converged on it, shooting up from below from all directions in a circle, to claim the prize. With a quick flip of its beautiful head, a 17-inch rainbow snapped up the fly, and the fight was on! After a nerve-wracking, but terrific battle, which more than made up for the whole previous morning, my catch and I headed home for a fish dinner.

I've since used the "firecracker" as an attractor pattern when imitations don't seem to be raising fish, and all else fails. It's a simple, easy-to-tie nymph pattern, but it can also be tied as a dry fly if you wish. I don't know the availability of the special thread, and I haven't seen it in any of the fly-supply catalogs, but I imagine the best place to look for it would be in a sewing or craft-supply store.

It can be distinguished from other "metallic" threads in that the two ribbonlike reflective strips of red and blue (I believe they're Mylar) are "twisted" around each other in a spiral pattern throughout their length. This results in a multifaceted, highly reflective surface. Despite this, the thread is of a surprisingly thin diameter, maybe .024 inch.

If you can't find it, never fear—you can make it yourself. And by doing it this way, you can come up with all sorts of other color combinations. To make "twist" thread, start off by selecting two contrasting colors of thin tinsel, of the type found at almost any bait and tackle store or fly shop. Take the two pieces and knot them together at one end. Tie this end down at the hook end to anchor it, pull the two strands taut, and rotate the two strands together between your thumb and forefinger, so that a spiral effect is created. You'll immediately see the results. Then simply work it up the hook shank—not excessively tight, or you'll ruin the effect—as you would any tying material, and tie it off.

I offer the recipe for my "firecracker" here for you, and hope you'll give it a try when nothing else seems to be working. Incidentally, it is a source of great pride for

The "Firecracker" Nymph

Created and tied by Jay Jacobs

Hook: Mustad 80259BR shrimp/caddis or similar, number 12 or number 14

Thread Underbody: cream or tan 6/0

Body: red and blue "twist" thread

Thorax: peacock herl

Head and Tag: a few turns of the underbody thread

The firecracker can be sparsely tied as in the example, or light-colored dubbing can be used to build up the body before tying on the twist thread.

me that the "firecracker" has been permanently included in New York's Catskill Fly Fishing Museum's millennium fly exhibit.

Jay Jacobs
Baldwin, New York

Hide Your Leaders

Camouflage your fly leaders by burying them in old, used, coffee grounds. Keep the grounds wet and the leaders buried for a week or more. Heavy leaders may take more time. Turns the leaders a nice, earthy, tan color and the shine is gone!

Wayne Mabus
Easton, Pennsylvania

Slipping Away

One day my best friend, Casey, heard a guy talking about the best place to fish if you wanted to catch a trophy lake trout. The place the guy was talking about just happened to be the lake Casey's cabin was built on! So, Casey decided to ask the guy a couple of questions about this place.

He asked him where to fish, what he used and all the information a person would need to know to catch one there. Casey told his dad about what this guy said, and his dad said, "We will have to try that the next time we go there."

Sure enough, the next time they were at their cabin they tried it. They went over to the sandy beach and went out about 20 feet and looked down. They saw exactly what the guy said they would. There were about 100 lake trout down there that weighed 10 pounds or better.

The guy said to use a big spoon with a perch tail attached to it and jig it around on the bottom so that it would stir up the dirt on the bottom. He said this would attract the fish, which it did. He also said to shine a light down to the bottom. That will attract minnows, which brings bigger fish. So they tried it and the next thing Casey's dad knew he had on a trophy lake trout. Everyone in the little tin boat started getting excited and Casey's dad, Bob, said, "Get the net."

After a 10-minute fight they finally saw the monster, then netted it. Everyone was relieved to get the beauty in the net, but it was not over yet. Just when they started to relax the fish started slipping out the big hole in the net. The hole got there because Casey always catches crawdads in it.

When Bob saw the fish slipping out he dove for the net and it tipped over the edge of the boat. Bob hurried and grabbed the handle, but the fish had squirmed out of the hole. Bob sat there in disbelief at how the fish had just slipped away and he'd blown the chance of a lifetime. When he finally came to, he tried to catch another one, but they were all too spooked to bite again. So I guess you should always have tip-top-shape equipment or be sorry.

Jacob Arthur Wichman
Great Falls, Montana

Pathways

The early fall night was clear and cool. A dark blue sky deep with endless mystery engulfed my world. Across the channel, maybe 300 yards away, cars zoomed by on the drive, causing tail and headlights to intermingle into a hypnotic state.

A light breeze embraced the small trees, rustling their still green leaves as ripples skated along the water's surface. My trance was interrupted by a loud splash in the center of the channel and I remembered where I was. I stood up and walked to the water's edge. The heavy rod seemed unbalanced in my arms. I set one foot on the rock ledge, grasped the long rod with both hands, reared back and then rocketed the weighted death hook into the night.

It flew far, landing only a few feet from the opposite bank. As soon as it touched water I began to reel and when I felt tension I reared back with all my youthful might. I repeated this motion a few times until it felt like I just slammed into a rock. But the rock wasn't a rock; it began to pull hard and my rod doubled over. I felt like I was being dragged into the water, but I held my ground the best I could.

A huge, dark silhouette exploded into the air again and again. Seconds seemed like minutes and after a hard 10 minutes I had the fish close enough for my friend to net it. We brought it to shore and laid it on the grass. When we shined the flashlight upon it, its size, the gleaming dark brown skin, its curved jaw and predatory teeth, awed us. Its eyes glared fiercely right into our unseasoned eyes. This was my first chinook salmon, and it lay there flopping in the grass, out of its realm, its side torn and bloody from my treble hook.

I felt sorry for what I did to this creature, yet I also felt excited and nervous. The adrenaline still rushing within me, my arms ached and my legs shook. It was a thrill to have this watery beast to do battle with, but I couldn't shake the feeling of what I did to it. It wasn't long before I discovered other means of catching salmon. I found more pleasure and satisfaction using bait and lures.

That evening happened many years ago, when I was in my early teens. I remember that night very well because it was a turning point in my life, changing my future for the better. I think of that night now as I travel on the drive, passing the channel.

I'm far from snagging these days. Today I explore the many tributaries of the Great Lakes, searching the currents with a fly rod. The rivers and its creatures have had such a great influence on my life, and it all started with that first snagged salmon. Salmon got my blood running to 100 mph, then steelhead to 200 mph, and the fly rod took me to Mach 1. This was the path that I had to follow in order to find the greatest pleasure in the simplest things. It's not hard to hate and discriminate against the snaggers we see today. If it's illegal and they know it, then let them get fined or arrested; most of them know what they're doing, and they will keep doing it if we allow it. There are those traveling along their paths and some may become the next great conservationists or well-known fishers to lead the next generation of enthusiastic anglers. One day you may read their books or watch their shows, while others will find their true passion for the outdoors, the comfort of waters and the love of our sport. In order to show them the way, we must be their enemy, but we can also be their road signs.

Josip Goreta
Chicago, Illinois

Editor's Note: Snagging spawning salmon was a legal and popular activity at one time, on Great Lakes feeder streams.

A Trip of a Lifetime

In 1995, I sent in $7.50 to the Save the Salmon Foundation and with this donation gained an entry into a drawing for a free trip to British Columbia's newest West Coast Resorts Fishing Lodge at River's Inlet. This was the opportunity of a lifetime, for the fishing there was supposed to be next to God. However what chance did I have in a drawing that had to involve thousands of people?

Well Lady Luck was shining on me. Early in 1996, I received word that I had indeed won this trip—all expenses paid for two persons from Vancouver, Canada. All I had to do was to get one other person to go with me and get to Vancouver. I asked Mel, a friend of mine, and he agreed to go. (You wouldn't think it would be hard to give away a trip like this, but it was hard to find someone who could get away to do the trip in the summer months.)

About a month before we were supposed to leave, Mel informed me that he could not go because of some medical problems! Now what do I do? My wife was not willing to go to a fishing camp and sit around while I went fishing all day. "No way," was her reply. I then asked my investment banker, Dave, and he said certainly, He would love to go!! There. Now, we were all set.

I had booked the trip for the first week in August and on time we were on the plane and gone. While traveling I always take my camera (and especially now since I expected to catch my largest salmon ever). On the plane I took my camera out to check it and found the battery to be dead. "OK," I thought. I will just buy a new one in Vancouver at the airport.

When we reached the airport there was not any place to buy this battery. "No problem," I thought. We will just use Dave's camera since we will be in the same boat anyway.

Upon departing Vancouver in a small plane, I asked Dave to use his camera so we could have a photo of the beginning of our journey. Wouldn't you guess it? His camera only had two or three photos left and we would have to be careful. I used two of the remaining three.

We arrived at River's Inlet and it was beautiful. It is on a lake that hosts a super run of king and silver salmon every year. Along with that, there were reports of large halibut out toward the ocean area. No guides for these trips though. You got your own boat and gear, but you are on your own as far as catching the fish. The first night there we took a boat out to get the feel of things. It was about an hour's ride to where the fish were staging their annual run. Once there we trolled for about 2 hours and caught exactly nothing. Guess there must be more to this fishing than we thought.

That night we were fed the most outstanding food ever imaginable at a fishing camp. This food would rival that of the top chefs in the world and there was plenty of it. During the evening the "Fish Master" told us how to fish for these fish. There was a special way to rig the bait depending on whether you were trying to catch silver (which had a zero retention law this year) or a king (which we were after). There was a two-fish limit per day of kings and a two-day limit (four fish) as to what you could take home.

The next morning we were off early to the fishing grounds, this time, armed with the knowledge we needed. Upon reaching the grounds we noted that most of the people were fishing on the north side of the inlet. After staying there for about an hour, we decided to try the south side. Now it was time to apply what we had been taught the night before. A wide roll for kings and a tight roll for silvers.

Naturally we both rigged up for kings. Within a half hour a good bite on my line!!! A super fish. The first one always is. I fought it for a while and Dave tended to the boat. A super job he did also. It was a king and a good one. Now it was time to get our lines back into the water and catch some more. We still had three more kings to go to get our limits to take home. I wanted a photo of this one, however, and we took it.

Fifteen minutes later my line went off again!! Guess I was on the lucky side of the boat! It was another king and, after a longer fight than the first one, we got it in also. Once more it was the handling of the boat that made landing this bruiser possible. Without it, I would have been hard pressed to land this fellow.

Back to fishing again. Now it was my friend's turn. He got a strike and I took over the boat. Wish I could say that I did a good job, but he was definitely better at running the boat during a fish fight than I. At any rate, we did get the fish in. It turned out to be a silver, however, and we had to release it.

A half-hour later, we did the entire thing again! The fishing was certainly going to be as good as we had been told. Too bad for my friend, but his second fish was another silver. Oh well, it's back to the lodge for lunch. We will come back after to see if we can get a few more kings for him as well. I kept everyone from our lodge informed of what is going on via our radio. I got the nickname of the "Communicator." I like it.

Lunch was as excellent as dinner the night before. What a feast!

Back on the water we decided to try an area closer to home. Well, it was great again. However, this time it was a king for my partner and several silvers for myself. I can only keep two today anyway. Evening time and back we go for another feast. Tomorrow we will try for kings again.

Tomorrow comes and it is off to the fishing grounds again. This time it is slightly raining, but that does not discourage us at all. The fish are already wet and a little rain will not keep them away. Once at the grounds, it is back to work. We have not been trolling for 15 minutes when I get another hit. Looks like another good day. This fish fights and stays deep. It has to be a king and a good one at that.

After about a half hour I finally get him in. We net him, and it is back to work. About a half hour goes by and we are ready to look for someplace else to fish. Too many people here and the fishing has let up. Lo and behold! Another strike on my line again! And to my amazement, it is another king! This one is the largest yet. Again my partner helps me and we get him in. I now have my trip limit and cannot keep any more salmon. However, Dave (my partner) still needs three more and we will work for them until lunch.

Lunchtime, and all we can do is to catch some more silvers. Dave and I decide to try for some halibut this afternoon and do something different. It is a different type of fishing and one we will have to learn.

After lunch we take off for the halibut grounds. We do not know exactly where that is, but we have a fish finder on our boat and we receive some verbal instructions on where to try. It is a ways in the other direction, but it is neat being able to see another part of this beautiful country. On the way down we find some more silver salmon and catch about four more of them. Now it is time to try the halibut fishing. It is difficult because we have to keep the boat in one position to fish on the bottom. Meanwhile, the fish are in the current! This means we should fish one person and the other should

control the boat. We do not do this and we are both in a mess trying to fish. It is a wasted afternoon and we do not get even one fish.

Tomorrow it will be back to salmon. I am determined that Dave shall get at least one more king, if not his full three more.

This time it is my job to drive the boat and Dave's job to catch the fish. After about an hour of fishing a good fish hits Dave's line. He brings it in and it is another king! Great, now he has two and is happy. We keep fishing, trying to get his other two, but we are not successful. We do catch some more silvers (wish we could keep them since they run about 15 pounds each and are perfect cooking size.)

Back at the dock we collect all of our fish for some photos. "No way," says Dave. His camera gave out also. The photos we took the other day will have to do.

As time will prove these do not turn out either. While it was a super trip, fully enjoyed by both of us, we do not have any photos to show what we caught. The fish are all cleaned and frozen so we just have to carry them home. It is a lovely trip home knowing that we have caught an enormous amount of fish and will be treating the entire family to smoked and barbecued salmon. If you ever have the opportunity, I would strongly recommend the West Coast Resort team for a super fishing trip at River's Inlet. It is worth every penny. My tip:

• Keep an extra battery with your camera, and always have enough film!

Michael Miller
Post Falls, Idaho

Go Natural

To my fellow NAFC members, my name is Jeff DuClos. I would like to share with you a story of a fantastic steelhead fishing trip. Within the story I will in fact try to share a few tips that I feel help make me a successful salmon, steelhead and trout fisherman.

In 3 consecutive years in the club I have earned a spot in the top 30 catch-and-release contest and then my 28¼-inch brown trout put me into the top 10 out of 1,811 trophies entered. My fish was caught on a fly rod and 4½-pound-test line; it weighed 13½ pounds and was released. In the year 2000, I entered 53 trophies in the NAFC catch-and-release contest, all caught on a fly rod.

Steelhead fishing is one of my favorite activities every spring. My destination is north to Wisconsin. There are so many rivers and creeks that run into Lake Michigan that you couldn't name all of them in an hour. With a little research anyone can find out where the better ones are, and when to go and fish them.

My favorite tackle is a 9-foot, 8-weight rod. I rig it up with a Billy Pate–Bonefish reel because it is light and has a great drag system. The drag system on your reel is the most important tackle element when you are steelhead or salmon fishing!

This particular trip, in early April, started out a disaster. My normal fishing area had water so low that I didn't even see a fish in over 2 hours, and that's not normal. I was forced to drive farther north to find higher water, and with that came the steelhead. In fact, as I crossed the first bridge and looked down into the water I saw 6 steelhead holding in 1 pool. Within about 20 minutes I had an 11- to 12-pounder tearing my line off of my reel, like he was late to his first prom dance. It turned out the fishing over the next 2 days was good, but because the water was low and extra clear it made fishing difficult.

My tactic was to switch to small naturals,

flies that resemble black stoneflies or black woolies; either one of these flies will land you steelhead when the water is clear, or when the sun is out. Normally orange or flashy flies work when the water is murky or deeper pools are being fished.

On this trip the number 4 short-shank black wooly was the fly of the weekend. It seemed that whenever I saw a couple of steelhead sitting in one place and not moving around, they would hit the fly. Having to fish with 6-pound-test line was a challenge, especially on fish in the 10- to 12-pound range.

With only 40 minutes left in the whole weekend I backtracked upstream to check out some gravel that I had caught fish off of earlier in the day. To my surprise, I spotted the largest male steelhead I had ever seen in my life. He was entertaining a smaller female ready to spawn.

I backtracked upstream until I could dead-drift my small black wooly through his hot zone. On the fourth cast he peeled off the bank like a fighter pilot looking for a kill. He crushed that fly so hard that I didn't even have to set the hook. He did two complete flips out of the water and then proceeded to run over 100 yards downriver, with me hot on his tail. I had to bring him into completely dead water before I could even think about landing this monster. Finally after about 20 hard-fought minutes he hit the net. My personal best, a 36-inch male with a 19-inch girth, weighing 16½ pounds. Not bad for fly fishing with 6-pound-test line with a 1-inch black wooly fly.

So remember, next time you're fishing steelhead in clear water or in sunny conditions, go to the natural flies—stones and woolies.

Good fishing.

Jeff DuClos
Ferguson, Missouri

True Fish Tale

Late one fall several years ago my wife, Trudy, and I were bank fishing for trout at American Falls Reservoir in southern Idaho, using nightcrawlers and marshmallows without much luck. A couple of other fishermen nearby were catching quite a few nice trout on shiner minnows. They finally quit and gave us three shiner minnows, so I put one on my hook and cast it into the lake. A few minutes lapsed, when I got a good strike, so I set the hook hard.

I told Trudy, "It feels like a big one!" After battling the fish several minutes, I got in close to shore and, to my surprise, I noticed a smaller trout was following about 3 feet behind the larger one, which I thought was strange. When the larger fish swam in a certain direction, the smaller one would follow.

After carefully netting both trout in our large net, we examined my lucky catch to see how it was possible to catch two fish with just one single hook. The larger trout had swallowed my hook, and the line had made several loops around the hard part protruding on the side of the smaller trout's jaw! The larger trout weighed 5½ pounds and the smaller one weighed 3½ pounds, for a total of 9 pounds.

Roy Abo
Paul, Idaho

Go For the Great Lake's Gusto

I never had an opportunity to fish Lake Superior until I was invited to join five others on a charter trip. We began the trip at 6 a.m. on James Maki's "Catch-A-Finn" charter boat. From the upper harbor in Marquette, we traveled about 43 miles to our destination near Standard Rock.

At 8:10 a.m., all of us were instructed to let our lines out, let them go until they stopped, then to start jigging and reeling. We were targeting lake trout by using a large white jighead, a double-tailed Mister Twister and a chunk of raw sucker. By allowing the line to hit bottom, create movement with the Mister Twister and entice smell with the raw sucker, we were guaranteed to catch our limits.

We started in 133 feet of water. On my third time jigging and reeling, I felt a lot of weight on my line.

"Oh, my God! I have a fish, Jim!" I screamed. My adrenaline kicked into overdrive. I had never fished in water over 50 feet before nor had I ever had this much weight dragging my line. For 12 minutes, I battled the fish. Jim gave me advice so the line and pole wouldn't snap. Jim finally saw my fish surface. He netted it, then brought it into the boat. He placed the net with the fish next to me.

"YES! All right! Whoo-hoo!" I squealed. I was clapping and doing a jig. (I look like a dork on the videotape.) Jim took the fish off of the hook.

"Cheri, come hold your fish," Jim said. I cautiously approached my first trout. I was tired and lightheaded from the fight. I carefully placed my hand under the gills, then hoisted up my lake trout. I was shaking terribly from the excitement and adrenaline rush. I had to put the fish down, then scoot it into the live well.

After the trip was done, I brought my laker to a taxidermist. After he weighed and measured my fish, he informed me that I qualified for "Master Angler" for 2000. My fish was 23.69 pounds, 37 inches long, and had a 25-inch girth. I received a "Master Angler 2000" patch from the Michigan DNR for this fish. In my purse are pictures of this lake trout along with the patch. This way, if anyone tries to dispute my love for and success in fishing, I have the proof.

P.S. All of us caught our limits using this bait and jigging method. We let about 10 fish go.

Cheri LaPointe-Kalisch
Marquette, Michigan

Letort Spring Run

The dog days of August were upon us as Jack and I met at his house at 5:00 a.m. We loaded our fishing equipment into the back of his old Chevy truck and headed for the closest water. Having secured our caffeine for the morning we headed west on the Pennsylvania Turnpike. As we traveled down the road the sun began to show itself behind us. Swarms of insects came with the sun, a good omen for fly fishermen.

Just a short walk down the path gave me my first glance of a true spring creek. Crystal-clear water with what looked to be a bottom of mostly clay. Patches of watercress were the only obstructions to the flow of water, which by the way, goes north.

This area is heritage trout water. No wading. I recommend waders anyway because the tall weeds along the stream will thoroughly soak you with dew.

Returning to the old Chevy, we made ready with our rods. We returned to the path and followed it, crossing the stream on a footbridge. We paralleled the stream for a few hundred yards looking for activity. As we moved downstream highway noise did become audible but it was not loud enough to be discouraging.

During the walk-along I was amazed by this shimmering stream. It was a constant flow of water, not the typical ripple-pool ripple-pool combination I have fished so often. While walking downstream I had not seen a single fish, not one! I knew there had to be fish in the stream and there are—educated and wary fish that at the slightest disturbance hide in the watercress.

We stopped for a while, watching the water and the air for action. Unfortunately no major hatches were happening just then. Jack and I decided to split up and work our way upstream. It wasn't long before Jack spotted a nice brown rising just around a bend in the stream. I approached as quietly as possible. Just as I came into position to see the brown rising it took Jack's dry fly. This native brown was quite impressive. The brilliance of its colors put hatchery trout to shame. Its colors were so bright they mimicked some redear sunfish I have caught in Chester Creek. The brown's pectoral fins were huge compared to the brown's hatchery cousins, enabling it to put up a good fight.

Jack quickly released the fish and we continued working our way upstream. I finally spotted my own working fish. I crept up within casting distance, I watched the fish for a moment until I was sure where I wanted my fly to land. I checked overhead for obstructions and it looked clear. I didn't want to have to stand up to untangle my line this close to a feeding fish.

From my crouching position I began false casting, stripping off line until I had enough to reach my chosen spot. "OK," I thought, "Let's just lay this puppy down nice and soft. Final forward motion and—Rats!" At the last moment my cast fell apart. Several feet of line landed right on top of what I had decided must be the trout's lie. The fish immediately stopped feeding. Jack and I waited about 15 or 20 minutes. The fish did not resume feeding.

It was late morning now and Jack thought we should go over to the Yellow Breeches since we were in the area. That was fine with me. I had never seen that stream, either. We headed back to the truck. Figuring that the shortest distance between two points is a straight line, we left the trail. Let me just say this; a straight line may be the shortest distance, but not always the fastest track.

The Letort is what fly fishing is all about: Wary native fish that are not overpressured (we saw only two other anglers that morning), but well educated—fishing this stream is the epitome of hunting your fish; casting to a specific fish instead of a fish holding area; matching their food staple and presenting it properly.

Although I missed "my" fish, the stream was a great experience. I will definitely be returning to the Letort for some more lessons. As I like to say, "That's why it is called fishing, not catching."

Charlie F. Russell
West Chester, Pennsylvania

This Belongs in Ripley's!

As a Lake Michigan Charter Captain for 20-some-odd years, I had seen plenty of strange happenings when it came to trolling for salmon and trout out on Lake Michigan. I have seen fish landed without being hooked. I have seen two fish hooked on a pair of treble hooks from a single lure. I have seen big king salmon, fighting mad, making a dash for freedom and running into the side of the boat, only to knock themselves out completely, to be netted easily. I have even landed a 30-pound fish that, after a reel-smoking run, just laid over and died. Probably the victim of a heart attack.

BUT! My most memorable experience out on the water should belong in Ripley's *Believe It or Not!* It was early on in my career as a Lake Michigan captain and I was guiding two couples out on the lake for a day of fishing.

Things were not "hot and heavy" but we were getting a few scattered fish. Suddenly the port side downrigger sprang to life with a 20-plus-pound king salmon fighting for its freedom. I quickly removed the rod from its holder and handed it to the young lady whose turn it was to catch a fish.

The battle see-sawed back and forth for about 10 minutes with basically no recovery of the fish; all the while, we were moving farther and farther away from what I thought would be the "hot spot." At this point I felt I needed to "intervene." I reached over and tweaked the drag on the reel just a little tighter, to gain better control of the fish. Well, as luck would have it, POW! The 20-pound line snapped with the sound of a rifle shot.

The young lady turned to me with daggers in her eyes. I thought for a sure and short second, I was going to be dead meat. But just as she began to say what I'm sure were a few strong words, the port stern downrigger came to life. I thought to myself, "Whew!! Saved by the bell."

I quickly reached around her and snatched the dancing rod out of its holder. I handed her the throbbing rod and commented, "Here, Annie, here is your fish back!" After a stellar battle (with me at the complete opposite end of the deck) the young lady brought the fish to the side of the boat.

Only then did I get near her, or her fish, and that was only to net the exhausted fish. I wasn't going to be foolish twice in one day. I was amazed at what I saw—it was the same fish! In the fish's dash to freedom with the dodger-and-fly combination it had originally bitten on still hooked firmly in its jaw, the fish swam down about 20 feet deeper, where I had a spoon attached on another rod on the stern downrigger. The treble hook from that spoon hooked into the split ring of the lure combination still trailing from the fleeing fish's mouth, and again attached the fish firmly on this other rod, to be eventually landed. Everybody was happy, except the fish, of course.

The crew was happy, the young lady who landed the fish was happy, and especially me, I was the happiest. I would never have to hear what she was preparing to say—or do—to me when the fish first broke the line! Here is my tip to go along with this story:

• Never run all of your fishing lines at the same depth while trolling for salmon, even if you are having success at a particular depth. By staggering your lines a bit, you will eliminate getting tangles and, who knows, maybe save the day on an escaped fish!

Capt. Herman Kunz
Fairfield, Illinois

A Great Day

It was a dark morning on this late fall day when I pulled into Leo's driveway. Time was 7 a.m. and temperature was freezing. I loaded my gear into the Tahoe. It consisted of cold-weather clothes; my Stanley, filled with plenty of hot coffee; rods and tackle bag, which contained all my hot baits and a few that were, well, not so hot nowadays, but were big fish-getters in years long gone by.

With a quick stop at the gas pumps to top off the tank in the boat we're on our way for the 1-hour, 20-minute drive up into lower Michigan. The ramp that Leo and I both like to use makes it easy to launch the boat. It's also in an area that has great fishing either way, up or downstream.

The river carries a name that is known all over the Midwest to many an angler, the St. Joseph River. Rich in history as a great body of water, it's as clear a river as any in the country. Smallmouth and largemouth bass, along with walleye, abound in these waters. For the last 25 years or more both Michigan and Indiana DNRs have built a big fishery with the introduction of trout, salmon and walleye. The river also gives up big catfish, northern pike and crappie.

The fish we were after on this trip is one of the best eating fish from the trout family: namely, the great steelhead trout. Most anglers who know this great game-fish know that when steelhead start their runs up the rivers along the shores of our Great Lakes area, the fun really starts.

There are all kinds of ways to catch steelhead. It just depends where one wants to fish for these wonderful fish. With the installation of fish ladders all along the way to Mishawaka, Indiana, finding a place to cast your lures is no problem.

Leo and I prefer to troll the river in an area where there are always some fish, even though we run the risk of being a little too early or a little late for the main migration run, producing what one would call a slow day on the water. However, you know there's always more to fishing for these trout on the St. Joe. Anyone who really enjoys what God made available to us right here in our own backyard knows just how lucky we are. Life along the river is just loaded with wildlife activity. So, a slow day is only measured as such by the number of fish caught.

Arriving along about 8:30, we prepped the boat by loading our gear and putting on the cold-weather clothes; then, launching the boat in the water, motor warmed up, we were off. We headed upstream from the ramp on the troll. We didn't need to go too far, as it's great fun for the first half mile, which has produced some nice fish over the years we have fished here.

We had no hits after the first 30 minutes, so we reeled in our lines and headed downriver for about 3 or 4 miles. One reason for the run downstream was to see just what the fishing pressure might be. If you're a big fish angler on the St. Joe, you know that there is a language used when passing another boat. Hand signals soon tell whether or not the fish are biting. We also get some idea when we see a charter boat working a given area. On this day, we only saw one charter boat fishing, and he was downstream just past where we wanted to start our run upstream. It seems that we had this part of the river to ourselves, as we didn't pass any other boats. This could be a slow day.

We spent the next 2½ hours trolling all the known spots as we worked our way upriver. Then it happened. Within sight of the ramp area I thought I was hung up on an underwater log. (Fact is, we were looking for this known log because today it was underwater, while most of the time it can be seen.) Leo managed to get his bait snagged on this log. I thought I had done the same thing, when I realized that my lure was to the west of the log in question. I noticed that my line was moving to the left. That's no snag.

"Fish on!" I yelled, "Fish on!" and I began to reel in the slack line. When I met up with the line I soon realized that I had one big fish on. I was glad that I was using 17-pound test wound on my 5500 Ambassadeur reel, and the 6½-foot rod with a strong backbone was a big help as well.

Now it was up to me to keep control on this fish. Ya'—right, keep control. I've got to be kidding, this baby had me on the defensive from the get-go. Just then this monster came up out of the water swinging his head from side to side as he hit the water with a great splash, pulling more line off the reel, even though I had what I felt was a tight drag; nonetheless, the battle was still on, and it was all I could do to play this beast with whatever skill I could muster up.

Then he came out of the water again. It looked to me for a brief moment that this beauty was a big king salmon. When it broke water again Leo got a good look at it and said, "That's a big steelhead trout you got there." "Wow," was all I could say. "If that is a steelhead, then that's the biggest one I've ever seen, let alone had on my line!"

After a few minutes, which seemed a lot longer at the

time, this fish showed no sign of tiring. My heart was beating like mad. My mind never even thought about my cold hands. It didn't matter much at that point in time. Now this fish made yet another run going under the bow of the boat to the port side.

I'm still just hanging on as the fish was still very much in control. Leo said he would prefer to net this fish on the starboard side if I could manage to make that happen. "Leo," I said, "Right now this fish is in charge—wherever he wants to go, that's where he's going. I'll hang on as long as I can, hoping that the line or hooks don't bend or break off." Just at that moment this monster made yet another run under the bow. This time to the starboard side of the boat, just like I had a lot to do with it.

Leo had the large landing net at the ready and, lo and behold, this fish all but swam right into the net. I dropped my rod tip down to give some slack line and the fish headed right into the net. Bagged, yes sir, he's in the bag. This thing was as large as the kings I had caught in the area just a few weeks before. Leo and I worked together to lift this guy into the boat. "We make a good team, Leo," I said. He agreed.

There it lay, all 31 inches of it. I put the scales on it. It showed 13 pounds. That's the biggest steelhead I've ever caught. Man, what a thrill. In looking up to see where we were on the river I realized we had drifted downstream several hundred feet from where we made the hookup. Fish is in the tank, time to retie.

We caught another steelhead about an hour later, upstream from the ramp about a mile.

Then it happened again. I thought I was snagged, but soon knew that I had another fish on. Fact is, I thought this one got off as I couldn't feel any pull on the line. Turns out that he was charging toward the boat. We did land this guy, which was more like the size that I had caught a few weeks ago. It was a 6-pound steelhead. With that, our trip was over. Leo headed the boat back downstream to the ramp.

Leo and I have shared many a year fishing together, and the only way I can sum up this day is to simply say, "Thanks, Leo. It really was A Great Day."

Jim Kehr
Middlebury, Indiana

Opening Day

Here's the scenario: At the time, I lived in southern New Hampshire, near Concord and Manchester. The month is April. The best part? Tomorrow is opening day of trout fishing in New Hampshire. So, I ask you, what would any person who loves to fish for trout be doing on this day? I would answer, getting ready for tomorrow morning!

Thus, the planning begins. I and a good friend plan to go hit the water at one of our small town's less pressured trout ponds, small, but stocked each year with browns. You may ask, a small pond stocked full of browns, with the possibility of some large holdovers from years past—why is it not under heavy pressure? Simple—this pond is on top of a small mountain. Only one road up to it, blocked by gates and rocks. No vehicles allowed, only people or anything else, on foot, can get to it. The distance? About 1 mile.

After deciding on our destination, my buddy and I head to his dad's house and load his aluminum canoe on top of my Blazer. All gear is now loaded, so we head to my bud's house to go over our opening-day plans and enjoy a little pre-opening-day cheer.

My fishing bud has to work in the morning, so we know we have to be on the mountain ready to go by daybreak, to have time to fish, not to mention hiking the canoe back down so he can make it to work on time. Pretty simple plan, right? Not so. My buddy, having the only alarm clock, sleeps right through it, waking up with only enough time to franticly wake me and run out the door hoping to make it to work on time. My thoughts at that time? 1. Why? 2. Ever hear of "call in sick"? 3. Now what?

My next thought

was, grab the phone! After a couple of calls, I found my fishing partner for the day. I had awakened a friend we call Davis (his last name). Half asleep, he told me he wanted to go out, but couldn't contact anyone the night before. Very quickly I told him what had happened, what the plan was, that I would be at his house within 30 minutes, and to be ready!

Davis and I managed to get to the trailhead within about an hour of my call, and began hiking the canoe and gear up the rocky trail. After lots of huffing and puffing we were finally there. Relieved? Not as much as we'd wished. Although sunny and clear, it was windy and cold! The pond had small whitecaps rippling across the surface. Small tree branches hanging close to the water had a coating of ice on them. And to add to our rather grim outlook on the situation, we were greeted by two other fishermen just coming to shore in a smaller canoe. "Get anything?" we asked. "Nothing," they answered, and added, "You're pretty brave if you're going out there—it's pretty brutal!"

Our response was that we didn't hike a canoe a mile up a mountain to bring it back down without using it. We did get that canoe on the water, and fished for close to 4 hours. We had some bites, but not many. When all was said and done, the canoe hiked back down the mountain and loaded back on the Blazer, Davis had the only fish, a small 12-inch stocky one which was kept for the pan as a reward for our efforts that morning. Although half frostbitten and hypothermic, we proceeded to scout out other fishing spots the rest of the day. When the day was done, we still had only the 12-inch brown that Davis caught from that awesome mountaintop pond.

A bad day of fishing?

Some would say so. Myself or Davis? I don't think so. Davis and I went—we hiked—we fished, on opening day! Yes, maybe we froze, but we enjoyed a day in the great outdoors, which I think is the goal of anyone who loves any outdoor sport!

Looking back on our opening day experience, I have learned a few things that are nothing more than common sense for anyone venturing outdoors, regardless of the sport they are engaging in. Since this story is going to NAFC, I'll just refer to fishing, especially on those bone-chilling days of early spring when it may feel pretty comfy in a lower, wooded area. However, if heading up to a higher area, or anywhere around water, especially if a wide-open area, these are my tips, whatever you're fishing for!

• Make a plan for the day: Extra alarm clocks are a good idea also!

• If your destination is walk in only, secure the lightest boat possible. Your body will thank you for this the next day!

• Allow extra time: If you think you can go from point A to point B in 30 minutes, allow 1 hour so you don't overwork yourself.

• Clothing, food and water: If you're hiking in, you definitely need food and water. Clothing: Keep in mind that if you're comfy away from the water or at a lower wooded area you will most likely be saying, "I'm freezing," when on or near the water, which can make for an unpleasant time, which is not anyone's goal when deciding to spend some time outdoors with Mother Nature, which makes me go to my next tip.

• No matter why you head out into nature, for any reason, plan and prepare for it. Bring plenty of clothing and supplies. Respect the nature around you. Don't leave trash, don't throw things in the water. Respect any and all wildlife around you, including the fish you catch. Ethical behavior is everyone's responsibility. And last, but not least, it doesn't matter what or how many you caught, it's about enjoying your time outdoors. I think you will all agree!

Shawn Collins
Newport Center, Vermont

Within Limits

Since many lakes and streams have a size limit, one has to make sure that the fish caught are within the limit. This usually required fumbling with a tape measure, tiring the fish even more. Instead of buying a stick-on measuring tape from a sporting goods store, I wrap thread at specific intervals along my rod in a color that matches the original wrapping. Seal it with clear nail polish, and you have a handy measuring system that doesn't take away from the look of your rod!

Michael Leger
Albuquerque, New Mexico

Another True Tail

We were still fishing out of our 17-foot tri-hull boat on Mormon Reservoir in southern Idaho. There are trophy-size trout and yellow perch in the reservoir.

I had caught a small perch that morning, but we were fishing mainly for trout using nightcrawlers and marsh-mallows without much luck. Sam said he would like to try some perch meat, so I cut some and he put it on his hook and cast toward some tules about 50 yards away. I surmised he was trying to catch perch. A short time later I saw the tip of his pole twitching, so I told him to pick it up. Before he had time to set the hook a large trout jumped in the boat between him and Trudy and lit in the motor well. Frantically I tried

to grab it, but it made one flip and landed back in the water. I thought it had broken off, but pretty soon I saw it jumping out of the water on the left side of the boat, so I told Sam to bring his pole around and fight the acrobatic trout. After playing the trout for a while we were finally able to net it. It weighed 3½ pounds!

Roy Abo
Paul, Idaho

Good Recipe
for Smoked Trout,
Salmon or Steelhead

Mix together: 4 cups brown sugar (packed), 1 cup salt, 1 tsp. black pepper, 1 tsp. seasoning salt, 1 tsp. garlic salt.

Filet fish, removing most of the bones, and cut in 1-inch-wide by 4-inch-long pieces. Cut the thinner belly part off the thicker part and place thinner parts on the upper racks of the smoker. Put dry mix on cut-up pieces, skin side down on smoker racks, and leave for 6 to 8 hours. Empty drip pan, wash out, and smoke fish until done. Smoking times vary with type of smoker used and outside temperature. Change smoker wood two or three times. If you prefer your fish a little saltier, cut down on the brown sugar or add a little more salt.

After removing fish from smoker, let them cool; then wrap enough for one meal in plastic wrap and butcher paper, or use vacuum sealer and put in freezer.

Roy Abo
Paul, Idaho

How to Catch Trout

o everything to a tee. (You can even catch native trout, just creep up slowly.) Here's how:

1. Use a very ultralight reel and rod.
2. Use only 1- or 2-pound line, no more.
3. Use tiny (size 10 or 12) hooks.
4. Sinkers—use small ones like .07 or .04 or around there. Don't use BBs. I think they're fly sinkers. Well, use real small ones. Get a size that just barely sinks your line very slowly with the current.
5. Bait—use only wax worms. Don't try using mealworms—too heavy. This is one of the biggest secrets, just wax worms. A plus is that they aren't fussy as to how you store them.

If you follow all of these instructions, you will soon know the way of the trout!

Floyd Charles
Center Valley, Pennsylvania

It Was the Fishing Trip from Hell

My boyfriend, JJ, and I were supposed to go up north and spend the Fourth of July weekend camping on Lobster Lake and catching togue (lake trout). But we got started hours late, and knew we would arrive well after dark, and probably would not get a campsite anyway.

So instead, we ended up at a camp belonging to a friend of his that I had never met. The friend was there with his wife, parents, brothers, sister, spouses, children, dogs …

The boys spent most of their time out in the boat trolling. Not enough room for me. I should stay with the women. They were certainly not welcoming. I found out later that JJ had briefly dated the sister's best friend, and the breakup had been ugly. (TIP Number 1: Don't expect the ex-girlfriend's best friend to like the present girlfriend.)

So, there I was, trapped. No truck, no boat, no fishin', no friends.

Now, there was a small sailboat that I had permission to use, but I have never sailed, and no one was planning to teach me. On the second afternoon I discovered that the mast and lee board could be removed and, Ta Da! A canoe. A heavy, slow, tippy canoe, but a canoe, a getting-me-away-from-the-bitchy-women canoe!

With my wonderful-if-you-stay-right-in-the-middle canoe (TIP Number 2: Bring your own boat), I paddled out to meet the boys, trolling back and forth along the near shore. I had to beg to get my fishing gear from them. No, Corey CAN'T borrow my rod. I need it. And the tackle box. Yes, I need my pliers. No, you can't borrow my Rapala.

I paddled to a small cove on the far shore, and amused myself by casting spoons for a while. About dusk, I decided to paddle around the pond. I switched to my

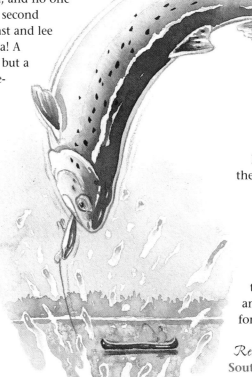

ultralight rod, tied on a jointed Rapala, propped the rod between my feet and set off.

Three minutes later, WHAM! The line started singing off the reel. I grabbed the rod, tightened the drag slightly and began to fight the fish. I'd reel him in a ways, then he'd spot the boat and make a run for it. The rod wasn't heavy enough to force him in! He would leap clear of the water, trying to shake off the lure. Keep your lines tight! He was under the boat. He was back on this side. The rod was bent double. I'd reel him in a ways, then he'd make another run.

Finally, he began to tire, and I worked him over to the side of the boat. One of the biggest landlocked salmon I've seen. Silver and sparkly. All that was left was netting him.

WHERE'S THE NET? It's still in the boys' boat. (TIP Number 3: Bring a damn net.)

Well, I thought, the only thing to do is gently lift the rod and bring him into the boat. And it was working perfectly until he just cleared the gunnels. Then he gave a last desperate shake. And the lure came out of his mouth and landed in my lap. I shrieked. (I am a girl. It's OK if I shriek.)

The salmon landed between my feet.

I paddled back to camp. As I pulled the boat up, JJ asked if I had caught anything. "Just this," and I held up my monster salmon. It was the only fish caught that weekend, and the largest any of them had seen come out of that lake.

They had been using the wrong technique. They had been trolling and casting. All you have to do is wait for one to jump into the boat.

Rebecca Manthey
South China, Maine

A Speckled Trout

In all of his 7 years, my son had never been this ready for a fishing trip. He dressed himself in a blue sweatshirt, hood up, with a yellow hat underneath. Instead of hip boots he put on his sister's old high black boots, as there was nothing else around.

His choice of rods was a rather heavy Ambassador he had used on last spring's flounder trip. The reel was Zebco 202 filled with strong line. A #12 bait holder hook was tied to the end, followed by a large split shot 12 inches away, topped with a huge red-and-white bobber set 3 feet from the hook. His mother drove him to the Hi-way Sport Shop for a container of nightcrawlers. He packed his blue tackle box in the back seat of my car. After saying goodbye to everyone, my son, Glenn, was ready to catch a trout.

We chose our spot. We drove to where the Musconetcong River passes by the Graphite Mill in Asbury, New Jersey. There are places to park on either side of the silver bridge. The river runs slow and bends above the bridge. Beneath and downstream from the bridge the river runs fast and strong, and tricky. We chose the latter, on the Warren County side of the bridge. We climbed down steps to the fast water.

In the springtime, the bridge is a tight veil of lines, fishermen and poles. The water is pelted with sinkers as heavy as 2 ounces. But on a cold winter afternoon, the bridge is empty. The river still ran low and clear after a long, dry summer. We heard no sounds coming from the mill.

We stood on a concrete ledge casting our nightcrawlers out to mid-river, then let them drift down. There were power lines above us and many snags under water. Within minutes my son had cracked his bobber, hooked a high wire and snapped his heavy line. Before long his interest was gone. He laid his pole down and began his explorations. My son found a box, which he filled with soot. He hunted for abandoned salmon eggs or other treasures. His face and hands took on the look of a coal miner. It looked like another of our many previous trips. Yet something was about to change.

My pole was an ultralight Plueger Summit. I was using a #12 hook, small split shot, and had switched to salmon eggs. For an unexplained reason my son put down his box of soot and asked if he could use my pole as his was without a hook. It was then I witnessed the birth of a trout fisherman. I casted for him as he hadn't yet learned to use a spinning reel As he held the pole, I told him to let the fish tap three times before setting the hook. He concentrated, held the pole steady and waited.

We both saw the pole tip bend at the same time. He hesitated then set the hook hard. My son reeled in an 8-inch brook trout at full speed. He released his first fish reluctantly. After another small brook trout, he landed a keeper brown. He and I cleaned his speckled trout in the cold river water.

That night he proudly carried our creel into the kitchen. His mother had already prepared a ham so he had ham and trout for dinner. Before he fell asleep that night, my son wanted to know two things; one, when would our next trip be, and two, how soon could he get a pole like mine.

Glenn G. Coats
Riegelsville, Pennsylvania

You Go, Girls!

It was late June and my husband and I were meeting up with several friends at our local favorite beach on "Walker Lake," located about 10 miles north of Hawthorne, Nevada, to get in some late morning fishing, afternoon swimming and lunch.

For the first hour there were just the four of us, two guys and two gals, each fishing with a different combination of bait, spoon, fly, spinner—and none of us having any luck. I learned to fish from Grandfather, who, at 81 years old, can still stand beside me in any creek or riverbed and pull out a limit of fish in 30 minutes or less and leave me empty-handed. Even though he has always been a better fisherman than I, he taught me the key elements of fishing.

1. They're either hungry and biting—or they're not—and you go hungry.

2. Patience. Patience. Patience.

3. If you don't get a bite in the first 10 minutes, the hole is either dry, or you're using the wrong bait.

4. Fishing tends to be its best on the worst weather days.

5. The more you want to catch a fish, the less likely you are to land one—and when you'd rather be anywhere else but on a hot lake or standing in a cold stream, the fish are abundant. But whatever the day, it beats working or yard work.

On this late June day none of us really cared if we caught anything, we were just happy to enjoy each other's company. About an hour into our fishing, our second batch of friends showed up in the boat to rotate taking us out into deeper water where you stand a better chance of landing a 5-pound cutthroat trout.

The guys in the boat were bragging because they had caught two fish from the boat launch on the way over and the four of us were skunked. The boat crew picked up the men in our party and left us women on the beach. As the boys pushed off from the sandy shoreline, my girlfriend had a fish on a fluorescent green ¼-ounce spoon about 15 feet from the shore and promptly landed it and held it up to show off to the guys on the boat, as this fish was bigger than the two of theirs together.

I changed bait and tied on a purple Power Bait rubber worm and about ¼-ounce weight and tossed my line—let it settle to the bottom—then gave it a few cranks. Strike! My lightweight rod felt like it was going to snap in two when the cutthroat trout made its first strike and then ran with the line when I set the hook. The men in the boat couldn't believe it. They were about 100 yards out in front of us using a new fancy fish finder. They

saw a few scattered blips on their screen, but were having a hard time actuating to them.

They came in toward shore a little bit to try and catch in our cache. My girlfriend was still fumbling with her fish trying to get the hook out, onto a stringer and back into the water. The fish that was on my line first struck when the line was about 60 to 70 feet out, but had since run another 40 to 45 feet. I was beginning to fear my 6-pound-test line wouldn't hold to get this guy to the shore. It took a good 7 to 8 minutes to wear him down and finally get him to shore. By then my girlfriend had tossed her line in the water a couple of times reeling in her spoon at a good speed. Fish of this size were normally only caught around the cliffs in the much deeper water (75 to 125 feet).

They trolled back and forth along a 100-yard stretch out in front of us gals. I had to cut my line as my fish had really swallowed down on that Power Bait worm. (Thank you North American Fishing Club. This was in a packet that you sent to my husband several months before and he had no interest in using them on the lake because "they wouldn't work out here." He has since learned trout will strike at about anything.)

By the time I set my line up to get it back in the water, my girlfriend was reeling in another fish. By now the guys had set down their sandwiches and sodas and all changed bait. Her second fish was a little bigger than her first. The guys bid us farewell, insisting that we were "bad luck" or had "jinxed" them, and as quick as that invigorating action came, it stopped abruptly—I think the fish followed the boat back out into the deep water—but they never caught any more than the first two they had when they met up with us. Those were the only fish we caught in about a 20-minute span.

At day's end, we gals were quite happy. My fish weighed 5.6 pounds; my girlfriend's were 4¼ pounds and 5.0 pounds. We rubbed it in of course and made the guys clean them—since that is the code of fishermen (and ladies) everywhere, isn't it? Those with the least, smallest or no fish have to clean the other person's fish.

As a moral to this story, which I guess goes back to my grandfather's finer points of fishing, I had been sick as a dog since January battling endocrine failure and felt lousy that day, but I didn't want to back out of our social commitment since it had been 6 months since we friends had gotten together or even conversed. The guys took our razzing, gave us each a big kiss and cooked up the fish in addition to cleaning them.

Walker Lake, Nevada, is a primitive lake and is one of

four lakes that once used to be one lake, 10,000 years ago. The others are to the north, starting with Topaz, then Lahontan and, finally, Pyramid. Topaz and Lahontan can be challenging as both are more directly affected by wet winters and summer irrigations. Walker Lake and Pyramid Lake have both seen better fishing days. My grandfather tells stories of when he first came to Nevada in the early 1940s, of catching 12- to 15-pounders—and, of course, of the one that got away, that he struggled with for over an hour, before it finally snapped his line on its final run out—he said it had to be at least 20 pounds.

Karen Best
Hawthorne, Nevada

Gotcha!

My son and his family lived on the Little Deschutes River, outside LaPine, Oregon. Their front door was about 40 feet from the riverbank.

My son and my grandson, Bryan, were dedicated fishermen and fished the lakes and streams in the area every chance they got. One day, my grandson was fishing right in front of their house, for nothing better to do. He had a small rod and lightweight tackle and was fishing with a #8 hook and worms. All of a sudden he had a hit and it was all over the river. He did not have any other gear with him, so it was just a wrestling match and luck. Bryan finally had his big fish in close to the bank, but when he tried to lift it out his leader broke. He saw the fish and his heart broke.

Bryan laid down his pole, ran into the house and called his dad at work. He was really heartbroken. His dad had to say something to make him feel better so he told him to go back, rig up his pole again and go right back after the big guy. He should still be around there.

So Bryan did just that. He tied on a new hook, threaded on a worm, and this time he got his dad's landing net. Back to the same spot he went. He fished it hard for almost a half hour. He was about to give up when, BANG! The big boy had him again. They wrestled around the river for 10 to 15 minutes. Bryan finally got him next to the bank and reached for his dad's landing net. He had him. It took both hands to lift him out of the water, but he got him, and back to the house he went.

He called his dad and told him. His dad couldn't believe it, but asked him to get his fish scale out of his tackle box and measure him. He was a big rainbow trout, 23½ inches long, weighed 3½ pounds. He had Bryan's first hook still in his mouth. Bryan was 12 years old.

Cliva C. McVicker Jr.
Beavercreek, Oregon

The Comeback

In August of 1989, my wife, three sons and I spent 2 days fishing with Capt. Rick Curatalo on Lake Ontario.

We'd been fishing with Rick the previous year and had had a very good time. Our biggest king salmon that year was 36 pounds.

We met Rick at Sandy Creek Marina at 6:00 a.m. He likes to get started early. As the day went on, we were catching king salmon from 24 to 30 pounds. We were fishing with downriggers and dipsey divers, and suddenly I had a hit on a downrigger. About the time I got the rod out of the holder, the fish was airborne. We could see it was a steelhead, and after a lengthy fight the fish headed for the boat, got in the downrigger cable and broke the line. Rick and I were standing there looking at each other, when my son David grabbed the dipsey diver line. Again the fight started; another steelhead. He brought the fish in, and Rick netted it. Then we discovered it was the same fish that broke my line. The broken line got wrapped around the dipsey diver. The fish did not hit the lure on the dipsey line. It was a 17-pound steelhead.

The big one that got away, but not for long.

Fred Hershberger
Apple Creek, Ohio

There Beside Me

I am not a scientific fisherman. There are insects that I can't name, and hatches I do not recognize. I do not connect my fishing successes and failures to the moon or the temperature of the water. Through the years, my fly selection has boiled down to several old standard wet flies. They are like the steps to a dance I can always remember, and can count on—they work for me.

Last summer, my grandson followed me along my favorite creek. He is 2 years old. The creek runs through a town. It is narrow with riffles, runs and some deep pools. I step into water and, above the noise of current, I hear: the town, baseball games, the speaker at McDonalds, car radios. After the spring stockings are over, I often have the creek to myself, and I know it like an old friend.

My grandson followed me through the grassy fields, imitating and chasing the Canada geese. He threw branches in the water and rolled over the bleached river stones in his hands. People walked their dogs, while others ate lunches or waxed cars. Everyone is talking. Everyone is asking, "How's the fishing?"

I start upstream where a walking bridge crosses the creek. My graphite rod is an 8-footer. My floating line size is 5 (weight forward); and my line leader is 9 feet long (6x). My first choice of fly is a hare's ear wet (size 14). No weight is added to my line. I vary my casts; directly upstream, across, three-quarters down. Sometimes I strip the line as if it were a minnow (it looks like a fish in the water), and other times I will let it rest directly downstream, forcing myself to wait … don't pull it in, not yet.

When a strike occurs, I don't have to set the hook hard. The small browns are aggressive and almost always hook themselves. I strip the line in with my fingers, slowly, then measure the brown against the palm of my wet hand and study the gold, the pinks, even the orange in their coloring. Most are about 7 inches long.

The day my grandson came along, I tried my other favorite flies: the Royal Coachman, Leadwing Coachman, Coachman. When nothing is working, I'll tie on a Wooly Bugger in green or gray and fish it the same way. My grandson got a glimpse of my favorite stretch of water, the one I keep coming back to. His big brown eyes with their long expressive eyebrows saw for the first time the fallen trees, boulders, places where water runs smooth as glass, the pipe. We moved farther from the people, upstream, and under the bridge near the grist mill. Still farther, where the creek runs swift and wild, and tears away the bank.

My grandson's knees were dirty. His hands were too. Then in that wild patch of water I hooked a fish. It surprised us both. It was one of the spring-stocked fish—a rainbow trout. In the swift current, it felt much larger than it was. It took forever to land. "Hold on, Conlyn," I said, "It's coming."

There in my favorite of all fishing places, I held the small rainbow in my hands, and brought it close to Conlyn. I wanted him to see its deep reds and blues. He was reaching as I was moving toward him. The trout flipped from my hands and was gone before he could touch the wet skin. I took Conlyn's hand and moved toward home, hoping that, someday, he will repeat the journey over and over—there beside me.

Glenn G. Coats
Riegelsville, Pennsylvania

An Unlikely Limit

It was a perfect day for fishing, typical of a late July day on the Russian River near Kenai, Alaska. I was fishing a deep run at the confluence of the Russian and Kenai Rivers. There was an island in the middle of the two, separating the crystal-clear Russian River from the greenish silty glacial flow of the Kenai River. The sockeye salmon were working their way toward the cold clear waters of the Russian River.

That's why this spot was so good. It is the last deep hole for the salmon to rest in before ascending the 12-mile-long, shallow Russian River. They congregated here in large numbers to rest, giving fishermen their best chance to target these fish before they entered the shallower clear waters above.

I was using a large purple-and-white bucktail fly tied specifically for the Russian River red salmon run, in an effort to entice the fish into doing battle with me. Actually, entice is not the right term here. I should say enrage instead. These fish have left the salt water, ascending rivers in an effort to spawn, and have stopped feeding. At this point, it is a matter of making the fish angry enough to hit your fly and try to kill it. The secret at this point is to find the color combination on a daily basis that angers the fish.

I was standing in the shallow water at the edge of the river casting my weighted fly upstream in an effort to get it deep enough to swing right in front of the fish lying on the bottom of the run. The fish were bright silver and averaging about 8 or 9 pounds each. Pound for pound, I rate the sockeye as the toughest fish to land on a fly rod that I have ever encountered.

They are electrifying! And, the food quality is superb, classified by the commercial fishermen as the best of the salmon species, no matter how you cook them.

The limit here on the river was three fish per day in possession, which many people found harder than it sounded to accomplish. This particular day I had already released about 18 fish from this spot and expected to hook and release quite a few more before the end of the day. The day began here in Alaska at about 12:30 a.m. and lasted till about 11:30 p.m., when dusk settled over the area. At this time of year, it didn't get dark enough to use artificial light while fishing. You could tie on a new fly and just keep on fishing, creating the possibility for a long, tiring day of fishing.

The day had dawned warm and clear and I was looking forward to fishing. Then the strangest fish tale you've ever heard actually happened to me.

I cast my fly into the head of the run, giving the weighted fly plenty of time to reach the fish resting near the bottom. The fly rod's sensitivity was the key to my continuous success with these fish. I could feel everything that was touching my fly deep in the river. Halfway through my drift, I felt a strange bump or strike. My fly had come to a halt, but instead of a fish catapulting out of the water headed downstream, it just stopped there and I could feel a strange pulling and wiggling taking place. I wasn't sure what I had hooked. I was having some difficulty getting whatever I had hooked close enough to identify. Other fishermen began gathering around to see just what it was I had hooked.

I was being careful with my strange catch so I wouldn't suddenly get broken off. As I slowly gained line on my reel, I could see a flash of silver deep in the river downstream from where I was standing. Suddenly, the strangest thing occurred. My fly emerged from the water hooked to the open loop of a metal stringer, to which three sockeye salmon were attached, each to individual loops of the stringer, each fish pulling in a different direction. This accounted for the strange struggle I had experienced.

Someone upstream had caught the fish, attaching the stringer to something on the bank in an effort to keep the fish fresh till he quit fishing. Somehow, the fish had pulled free of the bank and drifted downstream, still alive and struggling. As I landed the stringer with the three fish attached, a voice from behind me said, "Looks like you've managed to get your limit with one cast." He had never seen anything like this in all his days of fishing.

The fish were still alive, but they weren't in good enough shape to release. A game warden standing behind me laughed and said, "Looks like you're all done for the day." I pulled out my knife and cleaned the fish before heading upstream to my campsite. I looked forward to a tasty dinner of broiled sockeye salmon and time enough on my hands to tie up some more bucktails for the next day. So ended the strangest fishing experience I've ever encountered—a once-in-a-lifetime catch.

Tom Morrissette
Denver, Colorado

A Quick Escape

Last month, my buddy, "Fingers" Walden, and I were fishing the Big Salmon River for steelhead trout. It was a balmy 8°F, when we entered streamside. I was using my new state-of-the-art, 10-foot noodle rod, Micro spinning reel, and 2-pound-test monofilament line. (Amazing what a mere 45 years has done with fishing technology.) We were bouncing yarn flies along the bottom, in front of an ounce of lead. You needed that much weight to touch bottom.

Fishermen were lined up along both sides of the river, elbow to elbow. It wouldn't take long for me to clear a spot big enough to fish. Luck was on my side, because on the second cast I tied into a magnificent 3-pound rainbow. "Excuse me." "Fish on." "Coming through." I said as I nudged each person I came to out of the way. "Got to finesse this baby in," I thought, "Only using 2-pound test."

An hour or so later, I was back at my old spot, for the third time. Everyone around me was angry. (Probably because I released the fish.) The water was cold and my buddy, Fingers, was turning blue.

"How do you keep your eyes from freezing?" he said. "I just put them in my mouth one by one to melt the ice," I responded. "No you idiot, the eyes in your head," Fingers replied. I could see he was getting a bit touchy, probably because I caught the first fish. "Let's call it quits," Fingers whined. "No way, the fish are biting," I said.

Fingers left to sit in the car, while I decided to fish on. After an hour or so, my hands were frozen, and I could barely feel the line to cast. My brain was in slow speed, and I forgot to melt the ice on the rod tip. I

reared back to cast and heard a snap, as the hook, line and sinker shot across the stream. Some poor fisherman on the opposite bank was in the wrong spot, as the hook of the yarn fly embedded in his ear. The line with the ounce of lead then proceeded to wrap around his face until the sinker met him on the forehead. I heard a loud thud, and the guy was down. His friends ran to help him as I quietly slipped away.

Back at the car, Fingers was already thawed out. "You drive!" I shouted. "Had enough, huh?" Fingers chortled. "Let's get out of here," I said. "Where's your rod?" Fingers asked. "I've decided to quit steelhead fishing. I'm digging out my old telescopic rod when I get home."

Raymond E. Lemieux Jr.
Wolcott, New York

Ole Moe

Standing knee deep in the gin-clear waters of the South Platte near the little town of Deckers, Colorado, I watched as the air was filled with hatching Blue-Winged Olives. It was early November and usually these insects were long gone, but unusually warm weather had blessed us with at least one more of those special days most fishermen only dream of.

The morning had dawned overcast and about 50°F—a perfect day for BWOs. Anticipating the upcoming hatch, I had begun the day fishing a tandem rig consisting of a size 20 pheasant tail as my lead fly and a size 22 muskrat as the trailing fly. Experience told me there were some big trout in this part of the river and conditions were right for a good day.

As I waded into the fast, clear water, I could see several large fish feeding eagerly on nymphs drifting along near the bottom. I checked my indicator to be sure I was deep enough to drift my flies near the bottom of the 3-foot-deep run. I was using two microshot on my 6x fluorocarbon leader, hoping I would have a good drag-free drift. I tossed my flies upstream into the shallow riffle at the head of the run. As the flies drifted into the target zone, I tensed slightly, looking for the slightest hesitation of my indicator, a sure sign one of the feeding fish had picked up my fly. Nothing—I let my flies swing downstream before picking them up and casting back into the shallow riffle a little farther across toward the outer edge of the riffle, systematically covering the water in a grid-like manner. As I watched my indicator drift

slowly toward the feeding fish, it hesitated ever so slightly. I responded by lifting my rod and setting the hook. The fish rocketed out of the water and headed downstream, stripping line quickly from my reel.

It was at least 5 minutes before I could coax the fish close enough to tell that it was a huge, beautifully colored South Platte River rainbow. Within a minute or two, it became obvious that my 4-weight Powell rod could not overpower the huge fish while I was standing in this part of the river. I had to make a decision quickly or lose the fish. Looking around, I could still see several nice fish lying in the run. But, I knew I had to get to the quiet water near the shore on the other side. That would mean walking through the run, spooking the remaining fish.

As I waded carefully into the run, a voice from above broke the silence of the moment. "Looks like you've hooked Ole Moe." A homeowner standing on his deck was videotaping all the action. He had nicknamed the trophy he had been observing for better than a year, and I think he was concerned that I was going to hang him on a wall.

Once I had reached the quiet water near the shore, I was able to lead the tired fish close enough to get a grip on the tiny size 22 muskrat and free it from the upper lip of the huge rainbow. As I watched him swim back to his spot in the run, I think I detected a sigh of relief from above. "Ole Moe" would live to challenge someone another day.

This was just one of the eight fish I would release before the Blue-Winged Olive hatch finally came to an end. It had been like a dream come true, more than a fly fisherman could ask for this late in the year.

I was fishing with four other friends, but thanks to a little trick of mine, I had outfished my other friends 8 to 1. And so here's how, and my tip:

• Read this carefully. It has made the difference for me many times over the years. I keep four waterproof pens in a pocket of my fly-fishing jacket. These Pantone pens are used to break the outline of my leader in the water. I color a 2-foot section of my leader, alternating black, light olive, brown and dark olive. As best as I can tell, it effectively renders the leader material invisible to the fish. This little trick has proven its effectiveness time and time again. Try it for yourself and see.

Tom Morrissette
Denver, Colorado

Easy Eggs

These eggs are so easy. All you do is take some cheesecloth and cut it into 3-inch by 3-inch squares. Then you take your trout or salmon eggs and tie your egg sack like you normally would (two to four eggs per sack). After you are done with that process you will need a container with a lid that will not leak. Put your sacks in the container and pour cod liver oil over them. Let soak in cod liver oil for 15 minutes. Drain them. Stick in sandwich bag and you're off. Good luck.

Michael Levan
Buffalo, New York

Steelhead Fever

It was 1:00 a.m. on the third day of March. The weather was vintage Northern Michigan: 12 degrees and north winds of 15mph, putting the wind chill down to a biting 5 below.

Snow and ice covered everything like a blanket and I had the audacity to roust my wife from her warm sleep to depart on her first steelhead trip. Warnings of divorce were screaming through my head but I had been relating past steelhead battles of mine to her for a month and was confident her day would be spent on the river rather than in a divorce lawyer's office.

Carolyn is a firm believer in the old "I'll try anything once" attitude. She is an avid bowhunter and thrives in the wilderness. Our private joke is that she and I are the modern day Daniel and Rebbecca Boone. She had been fishing all her life but never for spring steelhead.

The night before I had indoctrinated her in the fine art of tying spawn bags and rigging the ultralight noodle rods for the upcoming campaign. I couldn't resist taking advantage of her inexperience (she knows better now) and put her through the ordeal of scrubbing her hands and then dipping them in tuna fish oil explaining the oil covers her scent. After tying 15 or so bags she inadvertently put a finger to her mouth and promptly began gagging. Apparently her taste buds didn't appreciate steelhead eggs. To this day I'll occasionally ask her if she is hungry for "Michigan caviar."

After loading the truck with every piece of warm clothing she had, we were off. Where we fish can get a bit crowded and you have to get there early to get the best spot. Not understanding this, she of course couldn't figure out why we were leaving 5 hours before daylight. She just assumed there was a method to my madness, knowing that I get a little crazy when the steelies start.

When we arrived at our spot and set up the rods, we sat back and waited for first light. To pass the time I recounted my memorable steelie battles and filled her head with images of monster fish trying their best to pull the ill-prepared angler into the freezing river.

I could see the anticipation creeping into her tired eyes and I prayed to the fishing Gods she would have the chance to fight a big steelie. Carolyn likes bass fishing but I'm convinced, pound for pound, steelhead fight harder than any other freshwater fish. They also taste the best.

Along about 6:15, we could see the beginnings of first light so we prepared to wet our lines. I gave Carolyn some last-minute advice about setting the hook and working the drag. She was concerned about the 6-pound-test line we were using but I explained that the noodle rod would absorb the fish's weight if she didn't tighten her drag too much. She seemed skeptical but also knew I had been doing this many years. So we threw our lines in and about 15 minutes later Carolyn's rod went off, her first hit ever. She grabbed the rod and set the hook like she'd been doing it all her life; her first fight was on! It didn't take long at all and her first steelie was on the bank. It was just a little male, about 5 pounds and I could see the disappointment in her eyes. Her expression was saying "Is that all there is to these things?" Here I had been telling her to prepare for the fight of her life and her first steelie was hardly an adult with little heart for a scrap. I tried to cheer her up by saying it was just a little one and wait for a bruiser.

We didn't get any more hits and decided to leave at 10:00. It was still real early in the year and apparently the steelies weren't in yet so we started pulling up the lines. I had told her earlier that she should jerk the rod every time she decided to bring in the line just in case there was a fish on it. Sure enough, she jerked one of her rods and immediately felt resistance. She thought maybe there were weeds or something on her line until it started to pull back. She yelled at me that she thought there was a fish on and then the drag started singing. I could tell by the bend in the rod this one was more hefty than the first one. Carolyn started screaming at me asking what she was supposed to do. The fish was trying its best to pull her into the river with it. I was laughing so hard I could hardly talk but managed to tell her to just hang on for dear life and don't slip.

After about 15 minutes she started gaining a little ground on the thing and her confidence was growing. The fish surfaced for the first time and I saw it was a beautiful female. As usually happens, just when Carolyn thought she had the fish tired out it made another run and just about jerked the rod out of her hands. The drag was screaming, Carolyn was screaming, and I was busting my gut laughing so hard I had trouble aiming the video camera.

About 25 minutes after she first hooked the fish she looked at me and asked if I would take the rod because her arms were aching from the fight. Not a chance! She hooked it and it was her fight, not mine.

Well, my wife fought that fish like a pro and we finally landed it. It was a healthy, wild, 10-pound 14-ounce female with no lamprey marks.

I took some pictures and gave her a big hug of congratulations. She just kept saying how sore and tired her arms and shoulders were but she had a smile on her face the likes of which I'd never seen before. She was hooked by steelhead fever forever now!

Our next steelhead trip it was Carolyn who woke me up to go!

Mark O. Hodder
Standfish, Michigan

Of Rainbows and Ice

We love to go ice fishing for rainbow trout here in New Hampshire and we are blessed to have an abundance of lakes to explore in our ice fishing adventures. Let me tell you how our family learned to catch rainbows while ice fishing.

All serious ice fisherman in New Hampshire are familiar with the annual Meredith Rotary Ice Fishing Derby which is based on our state's largest lake, Winnepesaukee, but is open to all waters in New Hampshire. Over 8,000 fishermen register for this event and it's all we talk about from ice-up into the weeks preceding the derby. We discovered early on that the best location to place your "bob house" is over shallow sandy bottom close to deeper waters. How do I know that these areas are productive? Do like we do, drill your holes shallow and just look!

We begin early after first ice, fishing smaller lakes that are known to contain rainbows. Many holes are drilled along the shoreline and in each several store-bought salmon eggs are placed on the sand. With patience and observation on your part, the tricky rainbows will begin stealing the bait. This is your chance to pull a switch and drop a baited jig. Be ready, as you may only get one chance at the easily spooked trout. Experiment with different baits and depths once you locate a rainbow hot spot.

Now for the tale of our first derby-winning catch. It was a cold 25 below morning as I crossed the lake in the silent and still predawn light. The family and friends were still cozy in bed after the long previous day's fishing. With little luck so far, they promised to come out a little later today. So I set about the patient task of drilling and tending holes, warming the bob house and enjoying the sunrise and sounds of other busy fishermen looking for their derby prize. I had been playing a cat and mouse game with an elusive rainbow on the previous day and all my instincts were telling me that there must be a big one nearby.

We were fishing Newfound Lake, a clear, deep and coldwater lake close to the derby headquarters on Winnepesaukee but away from the hustle and bustle of all the fishermen on the big lake. My friends joined me by 9 a.m. and quickly began kidding when they saw that I had no luck yet. Patience, I reminded them—patience and perseverance. I finally found the right trick at noontime while fishing a spring hole in 3 feet of water. The battle was on and the next 20 minutes were spent playing out our prize catch on the fragile 4-pound-test line we were using in these clear conditions. Everyone gasped when we iced a beautiful 4¼-pound trout. Now a second race was on, packing up our gear and rushing to the derby headquarters before the deadline to claim our prize of largest rainbow trout of the day.

That was over 10 years ago. We still attend the derby each year. Now it's my wife and two sons who do the bulk of the catching. Dad just enjoys drilling holes and watching the boys with their heads over the hole. "What do you see down there?" I shout. "Dad, come see, I just saw a rainbow!"

"Sure you did," I answer.

Richard G. Berthiaume
Allenstown, New Hampshire

There I was, lying on the ice with my hand half swallowed by this toothy monster. I tried to pry its jaws open with my free hand only to have that hand bitten as well. I yelled to Ken that it wouldn't let go. I felt helpless; every move I made, the teeth sank in deeper.

There on the ice he lay: 38 inches and 14 pounds of bad attitude and teeth. I was so excited at having won the battle that I hadn't noticed how badly both hands were bleeding. The snow turned bright red wherever I stood. I assessed the damage this fish had caused. I could see he had shredded my fingers, and bitten clean through my fingernails!

—From "Who Caught Who?"

Fish of the North

Two Pounds Apiece

On a Friday morning of a 3-day weekend in early spring, we packed the car with tons of fishing equipment including a Johnson 10-hp outboard motor with a full 6-gallon fuel tank, for an eagerly anticipated fishing trip to my Uncle John's place in Eagle River, Wisconsin.

It was myself; 13-year-old Dan; Stan, my father's boss; Hank, my uncle; and Frank, my father—all experienced fishermen except me. Everybody was from different areas of the country. Stan was from the South, Hank from Upstate New York, and Frank was from Minnesota. All my earlier years I'd heard these men on different occasions talk about their fishing experiences in Canada, Florida, Minnesota, the Philippine Islands, and so forth. I was always envious, in anticipation of when it would be my turn to sit around and tell my buddies about the big ones we caught and the bigger ones that got away.

The drive on the two-lane highway seemed as though it would never end. We arrived in Eagle River late Friday afternoon. My adrenaline really pumping, "Let's go fishing," I blurted out to a ride-weary group as we got out of the car. I got a pat on the head and a deflating, "Tomorrow morning." We unpacked the car, leaving the Johnson and fishing equipment in the trunk.

After talking to my Uncle John about how the fishing had been and what the weather would be, we got into the car and drove 3 miles into town for some dinner and window shopping at the two sporting goods stores to view the catch of the day. You see, back then each store had a commercial-type windowed cooler on the sidewalk where fishermen would bring their catch to be publicly displayed. One of the coolers had a stringer of seven large bluegills and three 2½-pound walleyes, which were caught on the lake we were going to be fishing Saturday morning. I was so excited.

The sun came up, and I woke with the first rays to shine through the slats of the blinds, got dressed and went down the stairs figuring I'd be first up. Wrong! There they were drinking coffee and making sandwiches and filling the old metal Blatz beer cooler. I said, "Is the bait shop on our way?" Dad said, "We already picked it up earlier. Let's go." We loaded the cooler in the trunk next to the motor and under the poles.

The four of us all seemed to close the doors of the Olds Ninety-Eight at the same time and off we went. In their cool way they hid their anticipation, but I knew they were as eager as I was. Ten minutes later we arrived at my Uncle John's friend's resort where he was putting the boat cushions (preservers) into the large wooden flat-bottom boat.

My dad hooked up the motor and fuel can while the rest of us loaded poles, net, tackle boxes, bait buckets and worm containers into the boat. Dad pulled the rope starter on the Johnson once, twice—I thought, "Oh ----! This clunker isn't going to start." But on the third pull, after some sputtering noise and a cloud of smoke, he shifted into forward, and off we went. I was at the bow, Hank next, Stan, and Dad steering. From the conversation with the resort owner prior to leaving the dock a few choice spots were selected to try first.

Failing to get even a bite at the first two spots, we decided to diversify our tactics. The water was calm, so we motored to about 25 yards off the south shoreline in the mouth of a horseshoe of weeds. Stan and Dad would fan-cast plugs and spinners while Hank would fish the bottom with a crawler. I would bobber a minnow.

After about 20 minutes of nothing, Hank started doodling his crawler up and down, up and down. My bobber had drifted close to his line. He started to pick up the rod tip to move his location. As the crawler was about to break the water, this huge fish comes flying and flapping out of the water, spewing mud in our faces, startling both of us back. The fish was within a foot of the gunwale of the boat. We both drew back, body and arms as one. Hank's worm was the target of the agitated fish, but because of the backward and up-and-down motion of Hank, the fish missed his worm, and on the down path grabbed my beat-up, limp, loosely hooked dead minnow, taking off parallel to the shoreline.

In shock, feeling slimy with mud all over my face and blinding one eye, having seen that mouth full of teeth, I hear the whining, rapid clicking sound. It was the drag on the Zebco 202 in my left hand. My right hand was wiping mud and slimy weeds from my face. Stan, Hank and Dad are yelling something like, "Set the hook, set the hook." What the hell did they mean? I'd never been fishing before. Evidently the question mark look on my face told my Dad I didn't know what this meant. He said calmly, "Put both hands on the rod handle and jerk the rod back firmly." I got the idea. It sounded easy.

As I drew the rod back with all my strength, nothing happened but this whining noise. The fish was taking more line as it continued west. I rolled backward on the boat cushion, bumping my back hard against the bucket of cement with the rope attached to it that we used as an anchor.

Suddenly the whining stopped. When Stan noticed this, he grabbed my line in his hands. Dad started the motor, slowly turning the boat west. Hank grabbed the net. Someone said my drag tension wasn't engaging and said, "Turn the white wheel on top of the reel." As I was trying to adjust the wheel, which just spun freely, Stan is taking in my line hand over hand. It's very quiet.

Dad, in an unusually quiet voice, says to me, "Reel up the line that's gathering on the bottom of the boat." Hank is holding the loose line a few feet from my rod tip with just enough tension so I could reel in smoothly. I'm sitting there cranking, thinking these guys are going to throw me out of the boat if I screw this up anymore. Over my thoughts I can hear the motor going from forward to neutral numerous times as the angle of the line in the water is getting closer to 90 degrees from Stan's hands. Hank says to Stan, "That's dangerous. If the fish decides to run, that line could cut your hands up bad." Oh, man, they are going to throw me in for sure if Stan gets cut, I thought.

"OK, ready," was the command from Stan. What, I wondered, was I to be ready for? My Dad astutely notices the big question-marked face of mine and explains that Stan will release his grip on the line and I'm to reel my rod tip down to within a foot or so of the water, then with both hands pull hard toward shore because there wasn't a steel leader on my line and the fish had a large quantity of sharp teeth. Dad said, "Don't be too upset if you break off the line." "Oh, sure," I thought, "after you guys did all the precision maneuvering, and gentle line retrieving, I'll just snap the line, set the pole down, and probably be thrown into the water with that bucket of cement." As I'm preparing to have the fight of my young life, I notice my line is stuck in the crevice between the oarlock and gunwale. I pull up a bit on the rod to unhook it, and the line starts coming out of the reel. No, I think I broke the reel. I hear Hank with net in hand say, "Do it now."

Thinking uncommonly quickly, I moved my hands up in front of the reel squeezing my hand white around the rod and line, then pulled sharply south and then up. I saw the net go in the water with Hank's 2 shirtsleeves following. I felt this strong force pull on my arms then suddenly the weight was gone. In my mind I could see the broken end of the line moving in the light breeze. I

opened my eyes and saw the net in Hank's dripping arms with this large fish in it.

The fish was a 31-inch, 9-pound, 12-ounce northern. "Not bad," was the overall comment in the boat. We headed the boat toward home, all feeling pretty good, but tired out.

As we motored to the dock, Dad and Hank were discussing how they should have checked over all the equipment, to make sure it was in good working order before leaving our home base. "Next time," was the comment. "Right now, we have to go back into town, put the fish in the display cooler and buy the kid a new rod and reel."

When we arrived at shore, the resort owner came over to the pier we were heading for and asked how we did? No one said anything. Stan looked at me and said, "Tell him." I half turned to the man and said, "We all caught a little over 2 pounds apiece."

Dan Augustine and Ken Kopier
Des Plaines, Illinois

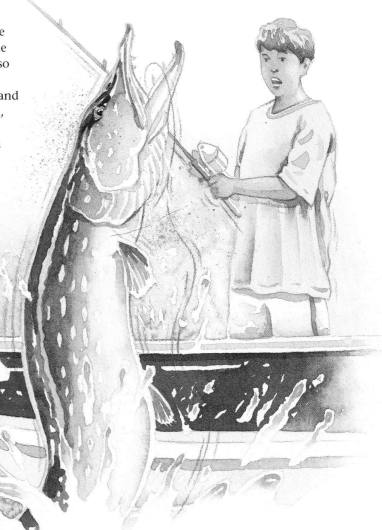

You Must Be Kidding

I had taken my youngest son, Christopher, on a fishing trip to Lake Des Moines, at Webb Lake, Wisconsin. Four other families from Washington, Illinois, were at the same resort.

One evening my good friend, Dan, and I decided to try another lake where we had good fishing earlier. Chris, who was 12 at the time, asked if he could take the boat out fishing. I had just purchased a brand-new Grey Thunder by Fisher Marine. Chris was experienced at driving a boat. This was before it was illegal for anyone under 16 to operate a boat without an adult, but I told him he could not go without an adult.

Dan and I left for the other lake as Chris and his friend, Ty, sat in my boat, trying in vain to get an adult to go out with them. Dan's son, Tim, said he would go out with them, but all of his tackle was in his dad's boat. Chris assured him that he had enough tackle to stock K-Mart and that Tim could use anything he had. Finally, Tim relented and rode with the boys.

Just before dusk, Tim threw a spinner bait into shallow water when something big hit the lure. After a long battle the fish came to the boat. It was a huge muskie. After seeing the fish, one boy went to the front and one to the rear of the boat and wanted nothing to do with the fish.

Tim talked Ty into trying to net the fish.

All I had was your basic bass-type net. On the first attempt, the fish was half in and half out of the net. Luckily it was still hooked. On the second attempt, after some coaching from Tim, Ty scooped it out of the water as Tim grabbed the tail. Once in the boat, the big fish flopped all around and Tim jumped on top of it.

Chris drove the boat back to the landing and they took the fish to the A & H Tackle Store to be weighed. On the way to A & H they went by where Dan and I were fishing. They stopped the car and hooped and hollered and ran about, telling us they caught a big muskie. Dan and I looked at each other and said, "Yah, right." We caught one small northern all night and thought they were kidding us. Reality set in when Tim said he broke my dip net and totally slimed my new boat.

I bought a new net and cleaned my boat and it was worth it for the night of fishing that those boys will never forget.

So instead of taking a kid fishing, sometimes it's better to let a kid take you fishing.

Tom Weaver
Washington, Illinois

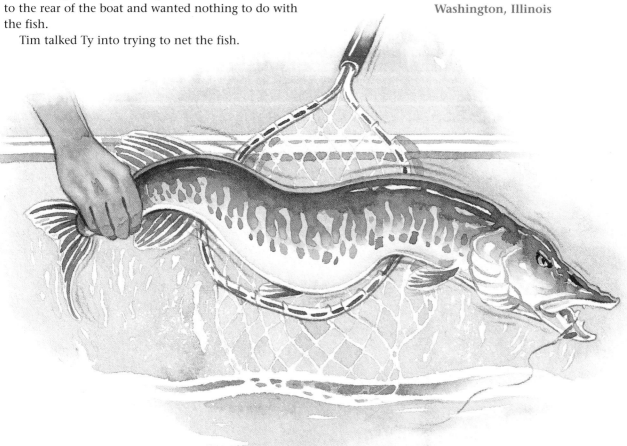

Hooked

In July of 1985, a friend of mine invited me to go to Snow Lake, Manitoba, Canada, on a fishing trip. I offered to take my 13-foot aluminum boat and motor and all my camping equipment. He took his 1-ton truck to haul our gear.

There were some other guys who also joined us; my daughter, who was only 14 years old, and two other girls braved the trip as well. When we got to Snow Lake, we found out we were actually going to Squall Lake. To get there we had to pull our boats upstream through a lot of rocks; then it started to rain before we actually reached camp.

We camped on a rocky island (try and hammer tent pegs into solid rock). My buddy had no change of clothes, so I think he was wet all week. We were all eager to get fishing. As soon as our lines went out the fish would strike (9- and 10-pound pike). There was no waiting! In all this excitement a fish hook somehow hooked the top of my hand. One of our pals had his surgical kit along, pulled the hook through, cut the barb off and back out. My hand really swelled up so he had to lance and drain it. Somehow I survived.

When the sun went down the mosquitoes came out.

My friends were comfortable in their tents, whereas I was still frying fish outside (mosquitoes and all).

One morning as we were fishing and they were biting fast and furious, I lost my dip net. Apparently there was some misunderstanding who had hold of the net, and so we lost the fish, stringer, dip net and all. To our surprise, I found it in shallow water just before we left for home. A fish was still in the net (just the bare bones, that is).

I nearly threw away my camera at one point; as I was leaning over into the lake, away went my camera, but again, I was able to retrieve it.

I wish I could relive this trip again, but all I can do now is remember it and share it with you. Northern Manitoba is the place to fish for northern pike and walleye and have the time of your life. My tips are:

• Always be prepared and carry a surgical kit.

• Always try to eat and clean up by sundown.

George Isaak
Shoal Lake, Manitoba, Canada

Secure Your Knots with a Match

If you're tired of your knot slipping and losing your lure and possibly the fish of a lifetime, try using a match as a little added security. First, after tying your fishing line to your lure, cut the line about ½ inch from the knot. Use a lighter or match to burn the cut end to form a small bead on the side of the end. Now the line will not slip through the knot. Remember this is just added security, so an 18-pounder just might slip through a bad knot, so do this with a polymer knot just for insurance. And, be SURE not to get heat near the main line, or you will weaken it.

Dallas Sprinkle
Huntsville, Arkansas

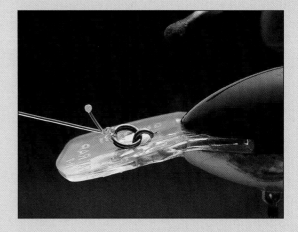

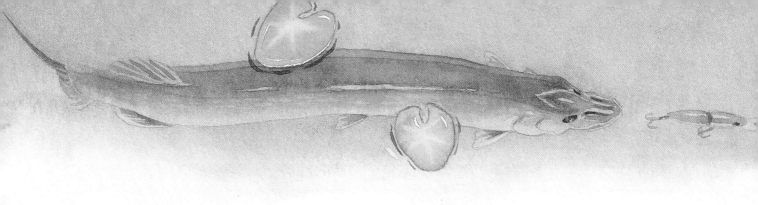

Enjoyable Fear

It began with intense anxiety and overwhelming excitement. It was my junior year in high school and my first trip to Red Lake, Ontario, Canada. The night before our day of departure, I could hardly sleep. I had thoughts of huge pike, record-breaking walleye and monster smallmouth. Needless to say, I didn't get much sleep. The morning came and it was time to load the bus. I never thought of the harshness involved in a 26-hour bus ride. Oh my! Halfway through I started wondering if it was worth it.

We arrived at the camp at mid morning. We went through all the rules and regulations, got our bunk assignments and our boat partners. We got dinner and got all set up for the first day of fishing and turned in early. The morning came and the fishing started. We fished as hard as we could in our 16-foot aluminum boat with a 25-hp motor. Without a depth finder and no maps or GPS, we were blind. We did our best, for a bunch of high school kids in a strange new world.

Our blind luck wasn't too bad. We caught dozens of small walleye and pike. We also caught two 12-pound lakers. However, we didn't get any of the monsters we were hoping for. We enjoyed the rough living of outhouses, no electricity and unlimited wilderness. As the last day of fishing approached, we were getting ready to swallow our hopes for a huge trophy, and get ready for that horrific bus ride home.

Then it happened; as the last hour came, so did our dream. I was casting a jointed Rapala, using a stop-and-go retrieve. About 5 yards from the boat was a huge shadow. It was following my Rapala. The shadow followed my lure all the way to the boat where I attempted the "figure eight." The shadow turned into the biggest northern pike we had ever seen. The pike came up to the surface, looked at my boat partner, then at me. He smiled at us as if to say, "Maybe next time," smiled and slowly sank back to the depths. We both stood there in utter amazement, our hands by our sides shaking in the most wonderful feeling of fear. We took a slow leisurely ride back to camp. We enjoyed the most beautiful sunset and shared the story with the other anglers around the campfire.

That feeling helped make the bus ride easier. Even now, years later, when I go to that spot I still get shaky and enjoy it all over again. Whether I catch that fish or not, I thank the Lord for the unforgettable experience.

Mark Johnson
Tiskilwa, Illinois

How to Unsnag a Minnowbait from a Rock

Open the bail and hold the line with your finger. (Just like you would if you were going to cast.) Then, you stretch it to almost the breaking point (1). Next, release it with your finger, and the line will shoot the minnowbait (or lure) off the rock (2).

Cindy L. Purcell
Laporte, Colorado

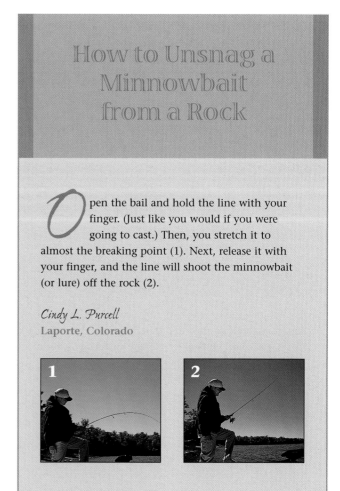

Hodag Challenge Experience

This by far was the most bizarre fish that had ever been brought in my boat. How this fish was landed is beyond any nightmare one could have.

It all started with my partner, Mike Brandt and me fishing the Hodag Challenge Fishing Tournament in Rhinelander, Wisconsin. At the start, everyone left the docks. We were the last to get checked out on the water. When we reached our destination, we found that someone else had the same idea as ours. So we then turned to plan 2.

By now, it was pouring rain and the lightning was pretty heavy. As we began to cast, we were starting to realize that this was probably not where we wanted to be. What we didn't know was that everyone had left and we were the only boat left on the water. The lightning now seemed to be right on top of us. As we looked at each other, we decided that just a couple more casts and we'd be out of there! About halfway into my retrieve, all hell broke loose. It was raining so hard you could not see a thing below the surface. When the fish grabbed the bait, it hit on the slack side of the bait as it was coming toward the boat. All I felt was a tick, so I set the hook and almost fell out of the boat. I was now reeling as fast as I could, looking at coils of line lying on the water. When I finally got the line up I felt the fish was still there. With the next hookset, I definitely knew I had a good fish.

Within seconds the fish ran into and wrapped around the trolling motor twice. With no more leverage, I threw the rod down and grabbed the line to fight the fish. As I was yelling to Mike to get the net, he seemed to have his hands full with his own problems. During all the commotion, he was trying to reel in as fast as possible. His reel broke and he had to pull in his bait hand over hand. Mike threw the bait on the bottom of the boat and ran with the net to where I was in the bow of the boat. The fish was now at the bottom of the trolling motor prop. This brute of a fish was pounding and ramming the boat.

Still not able to see the fish because of the heavy rains, Mike knew he only had one shot at her. So he made one good swipe down deep. As he raised the net slowly, both of us looking on in anticipation, Mike's voice broke the silence first. "Got her!" We both reached for the rim of the net and started to lift the fish out of the water. To our surprise, the rim would only come out about 6 inches. With the bait in her mouth, the fish in the net and the line around the trolling motor, we were once again between a rock and a hard place. I finally got the line cut and we pulled the fish aboard. I grabbed my hook-out tool and as I touched the bait it fell out of her mouth. After registering and successfully releasing her, Mike happened to examine the bait. The end treble hook was pulled out of the eye. The middle treble hooks had been straightened.

Mike and I ended up with a 40-inch female muskie. We tied for tenth place in the tournament. Lucky, you might say? Maybe. But I also believe there is a "Muskie God." My tip:

• First, not enough can be said about strong line, checking knots often and being aware of everything that is going on around you. Having a good net man is almost invaluable, and boat control is crucial. Undoubtedly the most significant detail pertaining to this situation was that I had put split rings on my hooks, then attached them to the lure. This allowed the hooks to swing freely and not let the fish use the lure as a way to pry itself loose. The fish just couldn't find a way to tear the hooks out right away. Also remember, knowing where everything is in your boat will help you to react to similar situations with more ease.

Bruce A. Kitowski
St. Joseph, Minnesota

Muskie Memories

It was July 15, 2000, and around 2:00 p.m., when I arrived at one of my favorite bass lakes. An overcast sky, slight breeze and air temperature about 95°F told me rain would be coming. As always, the anticipation made it difficult to get my waders on and lift all my gear and pontoon float tube down to the water's edge.

Besides being a good bass lake, this place also boasts a healthy population of jumbo perch, lots of rainbow trout and some big tiger muskie. All the state-record tiger muskies have come from this small 165-acre reservoir.

Soon I was on my way and headed to a large flat with a drop-off and two isolated brush clumps. I worked the outside edges of the brush with a ¹⁄₃₂-ounce 4-inch pumpkin pepper jigworm, 6-pound-test Green Trilene SX, and Shimano spinning rod and reel. I caught a couple of good bass about 2½ pounds apiece. Then, wanting to get right in the bushes, I switched to a heavier 8-pound-test spinning outfit and a 6-inch pumpkin pepper power worm without any weight.

I had caught three bass in a row when I noticed a father and his two sons fishing along shore, working their way toward the brush clump to my left. I set the hook into another 3-pound bass. Then I overheard one of the boys ask his father, "How come we aren't catching anything?" I let the bass go and headed over to explain the water they were fishing was too shallow and way too warm for trout.

That's when I spotted three 20-pound muskies swimming together just under the surface. That changed my train of thought. What an adrenaline surge!

I grabbed a rod without thinking and fired a cast to the cruising fish. The tiny jigworm was not my first choice, but something, anything in the water was better than the stupid look I probably had on my face.

The good thing I had going for me was experience. I've caught plenty of big fish on light line including an 18-pound northern pike on 4-pound test and no steel leader.

A muskie broke from the pack and began following my jigworm, came within 10 feet before it saw me and bolted. That was exciting and nerve-

racking. I wanted another chance.

I calmed down long enough to grab my baitcasting outfit spooled with mean green 10-pound Trilene XT and a ⅜-ounce rainbow trout colored Strike King Elite Tandem Spinnerbait. I felt confident.

Watching for another muskie to cast to, I noticed one of the boys on shore jerking his rod because he had snagged. The water erupted. Now I wasn't sure if the boys momentarily hooked this muskie or the line touched it, but here comes a muskie right at me which looked to be around 14 pounds.

Muskies exhibit a behavior known as "gulping." It's as if while swimming along the surface in a porpoise fashion they look like they are gulping air because there's no dissolved oxygen left in the whole lake.

I froze so I could see just how close the fish would get before it spooked. Well, it never spooked and swam

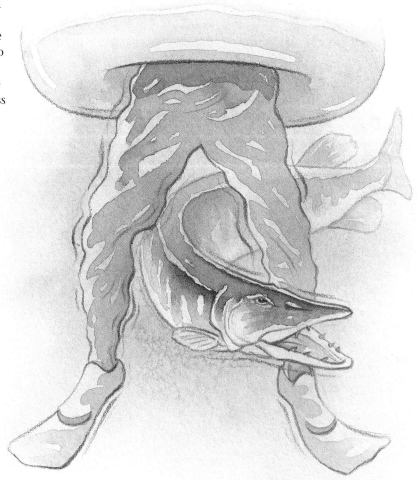

right between my legs!

It would have been easy to have reached down and grabbed it.

The father and his two sons saw this, as did a guy kicking toward me in his belly boat.

The fish was still in range; I thought a cast with my spinnerbait would get some attention, so I made a quick left-handed cast. Too short. Cast again, it's bulging the surface and their paths are going to intersect. They do and no reaction, nothing.

About then I realized the fish was circling back toward me, and I remember thinking, "It couldn't go through my legs again, right?"

I became still again as the muskie came around from my right. Closer, closer, until it's right under my pontoon boat. I could actually feel the weight of the fish as it "parked" right on my kick fins. The head was under the left pontoon and the tail under the right; all I could see was body.

The guy in the belly boat said, "I can't believe he came that close to you. I've never seen anything like that before."

What he didn't realize was that I was still looking right at the fish on my fins. I replied, "Watch this!" Slowly at first, I raised the fish with my fins and half-heartedly flipped the fish out of the water and touched the fish on the head before it flipped over the pontoon and continued on its way, gulping again as if nothing even happened.

It swam about 30 yards and submerged. I didn't see anymore muskies that day although I did catch 13 large-mouths, 23 perch and 1 rainbow trout. I know I won't forget that day, and I think the others have it burned in their memories as well!

Thomas W. Bonney
Aurora, Colorado

Quick Fix Reel Lube

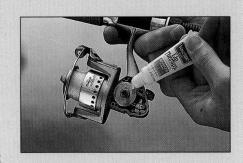

I fish in an annual pike tournament in Canada. One year, I was fighting a good-sized northern and the handle on my spinning reel became increasingly harder to turn. I looked for line hung up anywhere, but to no avail. I landed the fish and began to look for the problem. I checked everything, but found nothing! Finally, out of desperation, I opened the gear box of the reel. I was amazed at what I saw. Actually I was amazed at what I didn't see. There was hardly any grease on the moving parts, including the gears! After a quick search of the tackle boxes, I was disappointed when I found no reel lube! I carry a spare fishing rod, but I wanted to fix my "lucky" outfit. After minutes of deliberation, I discovered a tube of "Vaseline Lip Therapy" in my pocket. As a last resort I lubricated the inside of my spinning reel with the Vaseline. It worked great and my day of fishing proceeded with no other problems! Needless to say, I now check every one of my reels for lubrication at the beginning of every fishing season!

Greg Martin
Severn, Maryland

Catching the Cycle

It was the second week of August, but it felt more like October. The wind was blowing hard from the northwest and the temperature was struggling to get above 60°F. Standing out on the dock I heard a refrain that had become part of the everyday routine during our vacation to Stony Lake in southeastern Ontario, "… Mr. Herhal, can we go fishing on the boat?"

Turning to 9-year-old Nick Warriner and looking at the whitecaps moving across the lake and crashing into the dock, my reluctant response was, "Not today—the lake is a little too rough." A look of disappointment immediately covered his face.

You see on this trip Nick, his two brothers, John and Dave (ages 7 and 12), my son, Michael (12), and another friend, Brian (also 12), were my constant and enthusiastic fishing companions. Last year my 18-foot boat couldn't handle the entire crew, so the boys had to go out in shifts. This year, however, my new 21.5-foot fish-and-ski had ample room for all. Needless to say, the competition among the boys was fierce. Who was going to catch the most fish; who was going to catch the biggest fish; the inevitable conversation about what would happen if one of them hooked a muskie; and of course, who was going to be the first to "catch the cycle."

You see the boys had come up with a competition to decide who was the best fisherman. The first to catch each of the game fish in the lake (hence the term cycle) would be declared champion. For Stony Lake that meant bluegill, yellow perch, smallmouth and largemouth bass,

walleye and of course, a muskie.

With the wind blowing into the little bay formed by a point and the concrete dock that extended out from the cottage resort we were staying at (here comes the fishing tip), I explained to the boys that this is where the baitfish are being stacked up. I said to them, where the baitfish are, so are the big fish. Convinced that what I was saying made some sense, but still disappointed, they grabbed their rods and began to fish. A few minutes later I heard another familiar refrain, "… Mr. Herhal, I got a big one on." This was followed by the scream of a drag and the sight of a nice muskie leaping skyward.

Nick had hooked into the fish of his young life. After a few moments of panic, he began fighting the fish like a pro. Meanwhile, the dock that just a few minutes earlier held only the boys, was now filled with what seemed like everybody in the camp. After about a 10-minute battle, three beautiful jumps, and three failed attempts at landing the fish, the 34-inch muskie was finally secured in my cradle to the cheers of everybody who witnessed the event. After a few quick pictures the muskie was released to bring joy to another angler.

Armed with a light-action rod, a spinning reel strung with 6-pound test, a #6 hook and a worm, Nick's fishing dream had come true. The smile on Nick's face, when the fight was over and the fish secured, was unforgettable. However, there were no smiles on the faces of the other boys because they knew Nick only needed a wall-

eye to complete his cycle. Now the competition was on in earnest, with the older boys bound and determined not to let Nick win.

As fate would have it, I had promised my son, Michael, and his older brother, Matthew, that I would take them trolling for muskies. When conditions permitted, Mike and Matt loaded up the muskie tackle and hopped in the boat. Usually in August the muskies in Stony Lake are found deep, chasing suspended baitfish. But with the wind blowing and temperatures significantly colder than normal I decided to troll the edges of weedbeds on the windward side of several island groups (another tip). On our first trolling pass, using Believers set to run shallow, Michael latched to a big fish. After several jumps, drag screaming runs and what seemed like an eternity, the 46-inch muskie was landed, pho-

tographed and released. Michael had completed his cycle.

There is nothing better than sharing the joys of fishing with children. While John, David and Brian never completed their cycle (Nick did get his walleye), it only fueled their enthusiasm for return trips. I'm sure catching the cycle will be a competition among these boys for many years to come.

As a footnote to this story, upon hearing Nick yell "Big fish!" a cottager grabbed his video camera and filmed the entire event. Needless to say, the boys have viewed that tape countless times and Nick is the envy of all of his friends.

Albert Herhal
Pottstown, Pennsylvania

A Hot Spot

I was sitting on the bank of Lake Waverly, on a point, fishing with sucker minnows under a big bobber. Actually, I was lying on the bank almost asleep. I was on my second dozen minnows for the day. Being on my bike, I had to bike to the bait shop for minnows. It's 7½ miles from the bait shop to the lake. I love to fish, so I will go to any extent that I have to, but I was feeling a little tired so I brought my rod up next to where I was lying down. Fishing was a little slower than it was in the morning. I attached a bell to the tip of my rod and put it on the pail I used for bait. It was a long period of time before I got a bite. I was almost asleep when I did get one.

I got up slowly, thinking it was a bullhead (that's what I was mostly catching in the afternoon). But, when I looked at my line, it was moving fast. I opened the bail of my brand-new Diawa spincasting reel with my new Gator back rod. I wasn't really prepared for the fish that was on my line. I had 6-pound-test line with a steel leader.

I let the fish take line for about 30 seconds, then set the hook as hard as I could. The force that the fish gave back was more than I expected. I was expecting it to be a short fight before I set the hook, but after was a different story. It was a 20-minute battle. I timed it on my watch. I do that with any fish that feels good. It zigged, it zagged, and then it leaped out of the dead calm bay clearing 3 feet of air. I saw the monstrous pike. I knew the minute I saw it that it was bigger than my current record of 12.5 pounds. After I landed it without a net

and measured it, it was 27½ inches long with a 12-inch girth. To anglers who fish northerns and muskies, that is a baby. It weighed 14.7 pounds (I had my digital scale). I looked at it, looked at the teeth, the markings, then waded into about 3 feet of water, so the fish would have more oxygen to circulate through its gills, and watched it slowly swim away.

Now, the part that gets weird is that a half an hour later I was in the same spot throwing my favorite spinner bait that I have used for 2 years. I was ripping it through milfoil looking for a bass or another northern. I got a huge strike. Almost ripped the rod out of my hand. It was about a 6-minute battle. I was expecting to see a 'gator by the way it fought, but to my surprise it was a walleye. I couldn't believe it. It was 1:30 in the afternoon and I was in a 6-foot-deep, milfoil-filled bay. It was a 6½-pound walleye. It was the first walleye I had caught that season, so I had to keep it. The meat was like steak, thick and juicy. The best walleye I ever tasted.

Chris Forsberg
Montrose, Minnesota

My Greatest Fishing Thrill

In late August my good friends, John and Mary, asked me if I would like to go fishing. Now you have to understand that these people have never fished a day in their lives, and for that matter, this is only their second year of boating and camping. They have an 18-foot pontoon boat and love being on the water. John is 65 and Mary is about the same! My wife decided not to go.

Once on the water (Lake Marie of the Chain of Lakes here in northern Illinois) I started trolling with my two walleye rods with 10-pound-mono line. I was dragging a shiner colored SR7 Rapala Shad Rap, about 60 feet out, when its reel started humming. I grabbed it and thought I was snagged. I told John to stop and proceeded to reel in my line. It felt like I had caught a submerged tree branch because it was just plain heavy.

After asking Mary to pull in the other rod, and you know how clumsy a non-fishing person can be working a reel and how long that can take, I asked John to back up. Because I had commented that it was heavy, not fighting back and taking so long, John had started reading his newspaper and was surprised about my request.

When we were almost above the snag I started to lift and suddenly I realized and yelled that I had something alive and heavy. John thought I was pulling his leg. After about 10 minutes of back-and-forth retrieving I finally saw what I had—a muskie, a large muskie.

Mary had been watching over the side to see what I had and when she saw it, she hollered at John that I had a giant fish. John said, "Yeah, yeah," and went back to his paper. When the fish broke water and slapped its tail, John jumped up and threw down the paper. Mary was so excited she was almost running from one side of the boat to the other. I was afraid she was going to jump overboard to try and help me because they kept asking what they could do.

After another several minutes of playing the fish, I realized I forgot my net, so I opened the gate, got on my knees and gilled the fish into the boat. It was 43 inches long, but our size limit here is 48 inches, so after showing a few nearby boaters what we caught I released it, and after a bit it swam off. Looking my lure over, it had a bent treble hook and several tooth marks on it.

They wanted to try the area again to catch a bigger one, but I told them I've been fishing 50-some years and that was my biggest fish and I may never catch one like it again. I'm more into bass and walleye fishing. We fished for another hour or so and did catch a nice walleye.

Ten minutes after returning and telling my wife, we couldn't find Mary. She was so excited about our catch she walked to the camp store and told the owner, "Frank just caught a 43-inch husky." He asked if she meant muskie and she then strolled through the park telling everyone. Here's my tip:

• Don't forget your net and carry a Polaroid camera in your gear because most people think we're telling a fish story—maybe even your wife.

Franklin M. Herrmann
Palatine, Illinois

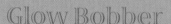

Glow Bobber

I make my own lighted bobbers by taping a mini cyalume glow stick to the tip of a thill-type pencil bobber. It's a lot of fun at night to watch the glow stick being pulled into the water by a fish.

Richard A. Worley Jr.
Oak Forest, Illinois

It Pays to Take the Wife

A lot of wives don't like to go fishing, but at our house that is not the case. My wife, Lisa, likes to go along and usually catches her fair share of fish. She never understood what the attraction of walleye fishing was, as she prefers to bass fish because walleyes are so elusive. On several occasions she went out with me and didn't do very well so she was pretty disgusted with walleye fishing. We fish the Susquehanna River in Sunbury, Pennsylvania.

One November day, we set out for another trip on the river and, on the way, I stopped at the tackle shop to pick up some shiners so she could catch a few bass while I waited for the walleye to come up to the dam to feed. While I was getting her rig set up with a shiner for bass, she decided to grab another rod and start fishing. Before I could get her rig ready she already had three walleyes on the stringer and had thrown two bass back in the river. By the time our trip was over we had our limit and had released over 20 keeper walleyes. Now my wife knows why I use Berkley Power Baits almost exclusively. For river walleye in central Pennsylvania, 3-inch tournament-strength power grubs do the trick, especially white, green and chartreuse and motor oil, which is the wife's favorite.

Terry LaForme
Ranshaw, Pennsylvania

Where There's a Will ...

Last year my friend Carl and I went perch fishing on Port Bay, North of Wolcott, New York. We were catching a lot of perch but had to release many small ones. All of a sudden when Carl set the hook on a bite he got a surprise! The fish on the other end took off for parts unknown. Finally, Carl got the fish to the surface and we could see it was a good-sized northern pike.

After the pike made several more runs, Carl got it up to the boat and, as I reached for the landing net, I got a surprise! The net was home on the garage floor. We had forgotten to put the net in the boat.

Carl asked, "Got any ideas how we are going to land him?" I said, "Get him alongside the boat again and I will put my fingers in his eyes (we planned to keep the fish—don't do this to a fish that will be released) and pick him up that way." (I had picked pike up that way ice fishing.) Carl got him alongside the boat and as I touched his eyes the pike took off. Carl asked, "What now?" I said, "I've got a pair of needlenose pliers; get him alongside the boat again, and I will grab him in the jaw with the pliers and pick him up."

Just as I reached to get the pike, my pliers slipped out of my hand and went to the bottom of the bay. Carl said, "What now?" I said, "Let me think a minute." Carl was sitting in the bow of the boat, an open 14-footer, and in front of him was an empty 5-gallon dry wall pail. I said, "Carl, hand me that pail." His reply was, "What are you going to do with that?" I said, "Just give it to me and I will show you." Carl handed me the pail and I said, "Get him alongside the boat again." As Carl got the pike alongside the boat, I took the pail and made a swipe, tail first, and the fish, 2 gallons of water and the pail landed in the boat. The pike was 32 inches and, after we landed it, a fisherman in a boat near us said, "I've seen it all!"

By the way, we caught two more pike that morning, 28 and 34 inches.

I guess where there is a will there is a way, and fishermen are very innovative. Hard to believe, but true.

Gerald Bates
Clyde, New York

A Perfect Day

What is actually considered a perfect day? There are a number of factors and conditions. Being with your son and best friends can be considered a perfect day. Lake conditions and weather conditions might be a perfect day. You don't have to catch fish to have a perfect day, but that makes it super. Catching fish is just that: an extra bonus. Did you ever think about it? Some people do better than others.

I have always been very fortunate ever since my father introduced me to fishing. It's always nice to have that divine power in your corner. I've had the opportunity to know some top-of-the-line lure manufacturers during my life and also some well-known guides. I've made some excellent friends with the Suick family and the Old Creek Chub Co. I met the famous Chippewa guide, Mr. Louis St. Germain. All of these make for that perfect day.

The story I'm going to tell you about happened one August, at the National Championship Muskie Open at Eagle River, Wisconsin. I was fishing with one of my best friends in our muskie club. Bob had never caught a legal muskie and I told him that this would change. The first day, we fished hard for 10 hours and never saw a fish. To say the least, he wasn't impressed. I said, "Well that's enough practice, tomorrow we'll go catch some fish."

The next day was the full moon and a cold front was quickly approaching. He informed me that he understood that cold fronts shut down fishing. I informed him that cold fronts can cause an adverse effect on the fish, but do the fish leave the lake? No, they don't, so we'll change our tactics and not give up the effort. As we all know as muskie fishermen, it is never easy and the fish don't always want to cooperate. But we have to think positively.

The majority of people fishing this tournament were pounding the shorelines to death. Bob and I had a game plan and we were going to stick to it, no matter what happened. He dug out his big weighted bucktails and I started with deep-diving crankbaits, like Cisco Kids and my favorite colored 10-inch weighted Suick. It was really unique, because 90 days before this tournament, I asked my good friend, Mr. Steve Suick, to special-weight this lure, and told him that if it was available for me to use, I would catch the largest muskie in the tournament on it.

Bob and I got everything ready in the boat and all or most of the guys took off in the opposite direction. He was getting anxious, as this was his first National. I said to him, "Remember our plan?"

The weather was perfect muskie weather. The wind was coming out of the northwest and the sky was very cloudy and overcast with a light drizzle. There was a good chop on the water. We began to fish the deep weed edge in 12 to 15 feet of water. Due to the cold front, we worked our lures deeper, slower and very deliberately to entice the fish. We were marking fish, but that wouldn't indicate that they'd strike. I can get my weighted 10-inch Suicks down to 3- to 5-foot range and the best part is that they hang for several seconds.

On our first drift, I noticed Bob wasn't making any figure eights at the end of cast. I told him to figure eight every cast. He informed me that he gets tired of making them. I said that due to the chop and water clarity, you have to. I barked back, "Figure eight every cast!" His next cast, I was standing there watching him making an excellent figure eight and he almost lost his rod. In fact, the fish almost caused him to jump out of the boat. It wasn't a big fish, but it was his first legal (32½). This is a catch-and-release tournament so we called a boat over to witness the release. This was the first time we met Harlan, Gordie and Arnie.

We went back to begin another drift over the same area. We had marked a lot of fish. On the second drift, we were approaching a 60-foot hole that was surrounded with a 15- to 20-foot shelf. Bob had another terrific strike and ended up with his second legal fish within a half hour. This one was 37½ inches. Harlan, Gordie and Arnie registered this fish, too.

As I mentioned, I had started with deep divers. I missed a good strike. I told Bob, I had better use my Suick that I asked Steve for. I told Bob to take us back into 10 feet and I made my first cast with the new Suick—and the world exploded in our faces. A muskie took the bait and went deep, barrel rolling, jumped out of the water three times, and a boat next to us saw the whole show.

This fish was 46½ inches and the largest in the tournament. The prize I received was a graphite reproduction by Joe Fittante, of Antigo, Wisconsin. This fish is on display at the Brodhead Memorial Library with a 6-pound smallmouth caught at the Nationals a few years earlier on a 10-inch Suick during a cold front and lots of rain.

Bob lost two other fish that were in excess of 40 inches. This all took place from 9:30 a.m. until 2:00 p.m. The end of a perfect day.

It was funny because some of the fishermen had asked Harlan, Gordie and Arnie, "How did you guys do?" Their remark was, "Not too good, we spent all our time registering their fish!"

If you really think about it, everything was perfect. It's a good tournament, you make new friends, enjoy the wildlife and it was a very enjoyable trip. That's what really counts, along with being able to spend some precious moments on our favorite lakes with our best friends. Being able to share what God has given us during our lives. The fish don't always cooperate, but give it your best shot, you have nothing to lose and everything to gain, and another perfect day.

As I started out, I have been blessed, and in almost 40 years of fishing, mainly muskies, God has given many, many perfect days.

A. Jim Heffner
Brodhead, Wisconsin

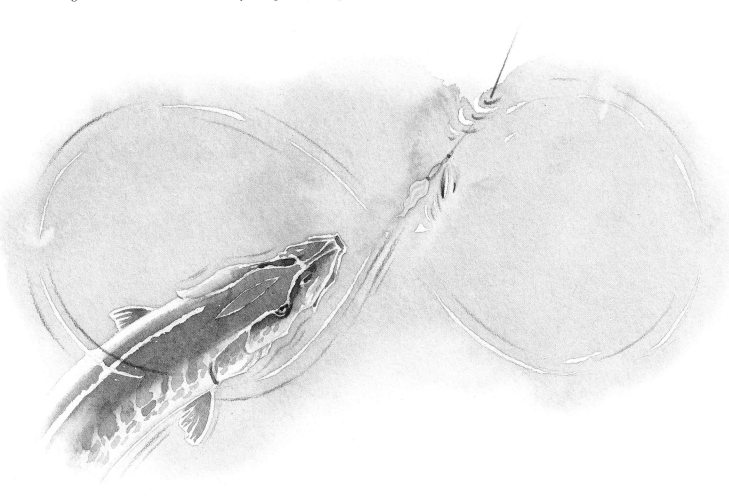

Searching for the Cherry on Top

The year was 1982 and my dad was getting the annual Canadian fishing trip together. Every year, I would help my dad get all his gear together and load the car in hopes of being asked to go along. I can still remember those post-trip fish fries and how everybody that went on the trips seemed like giants.

My day had finally come, the year I turned 13. This was the age in our family that gave you the green light to go on the trip if you so desired. My brothers, Don and Shane, as well as our cousins, Mike and Lou, had gone before and now it was my turn. I was not going to miss out on my first opportunity.

As an adult, I realize how much work it had to be taking a 13-year-old son along to Canada. We had grown up near Lake Erie, but casting and trolling were words that didn't sound anything like bobber fishing to me. That first year was a blast and I caught a lot of fish. I don't believe my dad caught too much for he was forever fixing my foul-ups. If you had looked up "the master of backlash" in the dictionary, you would probably have seen my picture there on the page. I did however catch a 15-pound northern pike that week and was pretty much hooked. My dad only had to hold the rod, tell me to reel and keep me from falling overboard, but besides that I did it all on my own.

Through the years, I have accumulated many fishing memories and that is all on account of my dad taking me on a fishing trip when I was 13 years old. My dad has been going to Canada for over 35 years and loves every minute of it. He enjoys the fishing without a doubt, but I believe it is the memories that are the "cherry on top" for my dad.

He went to Canada with his father and now he has passed that on to the next generation. I caught a 50-inch, 30-pound tiger muskie with my dad in 1996, and he could see the fire in my eyes. Here I had caught a trophy fish that my dad and grandfather had chased throughout their lives, and I had one. My dad was thrilled that he had taught me how to fish and I now had the ultimate prize: my trophy muskie. That was a thrilling day for my dad and me, and I think my dad treasures the memory of my catch more than if he had caught the muskie himself.

My dad was partially responsible for the muskie I caught. The muskie hit on a surface lure and put up a heck of a fight. It jumped seven times and the last time it went under the boat and jumped behind me. My knees were knocking and then I realized that my line had gotten snagged on the bottom of the boat. Of course, my dad saw what had happened and somehow managed to reach the snag and save my trophy. My dad deserves a lot of the credit for that fish. It's *our* trophy.

The following year, I was fishing with my cousin Mike, and I was acting as the guide for the day. Mike and I had become pretty close due in part to these fishing trips and now we were hunting trophy muskie together. Mike is an excellent fisherman and was in search of a trophy. We ended up having a great time fishing and 3 hours later we had a 48-inch muskie in the boat, courtesy of Mike. I felt a sort of pride that we had done what we had set out to do. We had all set out to catch big muskie that day and, when it happened, the sense of accomplishment was almost overwhelming. I also felt a sense of what my dad did when I caught my muskie. To see the look in my cousin's eyes when he caught his muskie was very special for me. I know my dad had to feel the same way on our special day in 1996.

In 1998, I was fishing with my oldest brother, Don, and he is obsessed with muskie. He is an excellent fisherman, which I attribute to his teacher, our dad. Don, however, believes he has to get all kinds of fanatical gear to increase the odds of catching a big muskie.

On this trip, I was fishing with my brother a lot because we both like to cast and our dad loves to troll. We came to an area and started seeing some action. Don had a major hit on a surface lure, but the fish missed the bait. The activity of the fish turned off and Don suggested we should leave the area for a while.

Leaving that bay, we knew that big fish were there and that we would return. We decided to find our dad and take him there in hopes that he could catch a BIG ONE. Our dad followed us to the bay and, three casts later, I had another nice muskie on my line. Once again this muskie hit a surface bait and fought violently to get away. We landed the fish and, once again, I fully understood the desire to catch one of these awesome fish. My dad had a front row seat for the catch and gave me the thumbs up on a really nice catch. I believe this was

another "cherry on top" for my dad.

In 2000, I was unable to go on the trip with my dad and I missed the new memories. My dad, however, did go and is still searching for his muskie. This year we are headed to a new camp farther north in Ontario, so my dad can continue his lifelong quest for a trophy muskie.

I believe that, even if my dad doesn't catch his trophy muskie he wouldn't have traded the journey and experiences with anyone. This year it is my dad, my brother Don, my cousin Mike and I who are making the "MUSKIE" trip to Canada. Everyone will be looking forward to catching a big one. I, on the other hand, have a different agenda. My dad has seen the special look in my eyes after catching both of my muskies. I have seen a similar look in my cousin's eyes when he caught his trophy. My dad has caught many muskies, but he hasn't found his trophy. I am in search of that look in my dad's eyes when he catches his MUSKIE. That will be my "cherry on top." So here's my tip:

• Enjoy the day. You can have all the equipment you need, all the necessary skills, the desire to always have a successful day fishing. But I believe that catching anything is secondary. You need to enjoy the time you have to fish with the people that also love to wet a line. Believe me when I tell you that if you should catch anything at all, it will be a "cherry on top."

Thomas W. Vogel
Blanchester, Ohio

Grandma's Catch

To begin this story, I will tell that I am a retired grandmother with 25 grandkids. Until the last few years, there wasn't much time for fishing, but I started taking some of the grandkids to some of the local ponds and the river. We caught some panfish and a few channel cats, but never any big ones or, as I say, "gamefish."

Two years ago some of our children decided to take a 4-day weekend at a resort in northern Wisconsin, and Mom and Dad were to come along. The first morning I was fishing with one of my sons, we were throwing crankbaits and weedless lures.

We had a few strikes, when my son said to me, "Mom, you'll never get a muskie out of here unless you have 50-pound-test line on your reel." The weeds were very thick.

That same evening my daughter and grandson wanted to fish with me, so we headed to the same spot. We caught a few perch and suddenly they stopped biting. The sun was going down so I thought, before we leave, I'm going to try a few casts with a weedless lure. The second cast was the hit. He came to the surface and broke out of the water, so we could see it was a good-sized fish. My grandson was bringing in the extra lines and the anchor, and my daughter was ready with the net. I said, "Forget it. We'll never get him in the boat." I was fishing with 8-pound-test line. I got him to the boat twice. And the third time she netted the 37½-inch muskie. We were all shaking, it was so exciting. Naturally Grandma was the fisherman of the day, and we did release it.

• Always fish with someone who can give you help; without my daughter I never would have gotten that fish in the boat. My son had to eat some crow, and I'm still trying for the one I can mount on the wall.

Kathy Weinfurter
Rudolph, Wisconsin

Who Caught Who?

It was a beautiful winter day in Cicero, New York. A 3-inch fluffy snow had fallen overnight. Looking out over Oneida Lake I could see some ice fishermen heading to their spots. They appeared as tiny dots moving against a bright white background. Six to seven inches of ice covered the lake, making it safe to venture out by snowmobile. I had purchased bait, checked over my equipment and gassed up the sled the previous day. I was ready for my first ice-fishing outing of the season.

On the second pull the engine in my old 1980 Polaris began to purr. I wouldn't be walking today. I grabbed my gear and headed to a drop-off in front of our house. I knew this area held perch and an occasional walleye at early ice. I found a buoy, poking through the lake, that marked the location of an underwater rock wall. The depth changed quickly from 3 to 12 feet just past the buoy. This was the spot to make my first holes.

My wife had given me a new 6-inch Lazer ice auger for Christmas. I began drilling through the ice, and was amazed at how fast and easy it cut. "Thanks, Honey," I thought. I had punched two holes in no time. I baited two ice dots with 2-inch minnows hooked through the lips, and free-spooled them to the lake bottom. A couple of turns on each ultralight reel brought the bait 4 inches off bottom. I propped both poles and observed the rod tips pulsing slightly from the minnows' struggle below the ice. When the minnows became lethargic a little jig would get them swimming again. Nothing to do now but sit back and wait for a bite.

I had been fishing for half an hour when I noticed a figure dressed in orange walking toward me. He stopped when he got to me and asked how the fish were biting. "So far nothing," I responded. He introduced himself as Ken, and asked if I minded if he fished nearby. I was happy to have someone to make conversation with since the fish weren't cooperating. We exchanged small talk for awhile, when I looked down and saw one of my poles begin to flex. "There's one," I said to Ken. I set the hook and was startled when the drag on my reel began screaming. I knew immediately this wasn't a perch or walleye. Whatever it was, it stripped line like no fish I had ever hooked through hard water. As the fish continued its run for freedom I looked down to see my 4-pound-test line rubbing against the ice edge. I knew my light line would be cut easily by the sharp ice if the fish continued its run.

Quickly, I plunged the pole down the hole to avoid the line's contact with the ice. Gradually the fish began to slow, then stop. I was steadily gaining line now. I had

about half my line back when the fish took off on another dash. Again I submerged my pole until the fish halted its run. This whole process repeated itself for about 15 minutes, when I heard Ken say, "I've got to see this."

As he approached we wondered, out loud, what I had on the end of my line—catfish, carp, big brown trout? Twenty minutes had now passed, and we hadn't seen the fish. Ken joked that he should have timed me. We discussed the possibility of it being a northern pike, but decided a Northern's teeth would have cut my line after so many runs. I was shaking with excitement, and dying to see what I had hooked.

The fish's sprints were getting shorter now. I was gaining line after each run. Finally, I was about to see this mystery fish. As I brought the fish closer, I peered into the hole, hoping for a glimpse of what had taken my bait. Suddenly there was a green flash just under the ice. The mystery was no more. This was a huge northern pike. Ken and I gasped when we saw the size of this hard-fighting fish. After a couple more short runs the fish came to rest at the base of the hole.

I could see my line protruding from the corner of this giant's mouth, its teeth not quite touching the monofilament. I grabbed the line and ever so gently tried to guide his snout into the hole. I only succeeded in bumping his head under the ice. This angered the fish and he was off on yet another run. The bump-and-run repeated itself a couple of times when we realized the fish wouldn't stick its head in the hole for us.

Ken and I debated about drilling another hole right next to the existing one so we could land this fish. We decided against it. My light line in such close proximity to sharp auger blades meant certain defeat. I had two options. Cut the line and watch him swim away, or go in after him. I wasn't about to let him go, so I pulled up my sleeve and thrust my bare hand into the icy water.

I was feeling for the gill plate to grab when I felt the sharp pain of what seemed like hundreds of tiny needles deeply piercing my skin. I had misjudged and stuck my hand into this 'gator's mouth! I tried to shake him off, but he wouldn't release his grip. Each time I shook my hand I could feel his teeth rip and tear. I had to get my arm out of the water.

As I withdrew my arm the fish came with it, refusing to let go. When his head emerged, I grabbed his gill plate with my other hand and pulled. About halfway out of the hole the fish became wedged. It took some force to get him through the 6-inch circular opening.

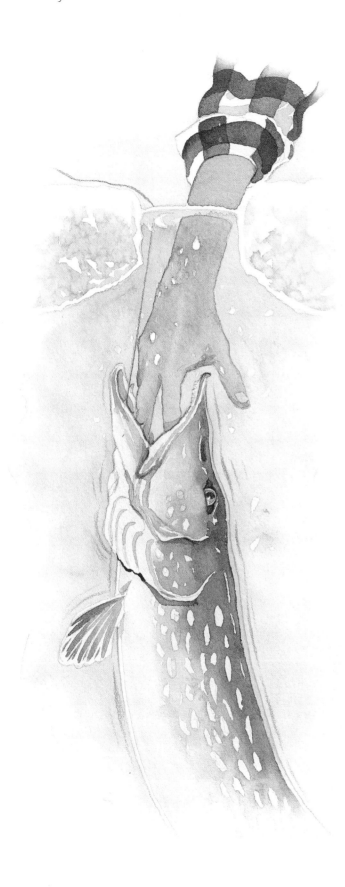

Finally I had him on the ice, or should I say he had me.

There I was, lying on the ice with my hand half swallowed by this toothy monster. I tried to pry its jaws open with my free hand only to have that hand bitten as well. I yelled to Ken that it wouldn't let go. I felt helpless; every move I made, the teeth sank in deeper. Ken used both his gloved hands to pry the northern's jaws apart and I slid my hand from its grasp. Just as my hand was clear the fish bit down on Ken's gloves poking numerous holes in the leather. Now it had Ken. I used needlenose pliers to leverage the fish's mouth open and Ken's hands were free.

There on the ice he lay: 38 inches and 14 pounds of bad attitude and teeth. I was so excited at having won the battle that I hadn't noticed how badly both hands were bleeding. The snow turned bright red wherever I stood. I assessed the damage this fish had caused. I could see he had shredded my fingers, and bitten clean through my fingernails! I thanked Ken for his help and hurried home to stop the bleeding, my trophy draped across my lap.

After applying 15 bandages to my wounds, I went to see the doctor. Doc cleaned me up as I told him my story. He seemed to enjoy the tale, being a fisherman himself.

Now this beautiful specimen hangs on my wall. I learned that he was approximately 15 years old, and one of the largest great northern pike to come from Oneida Lake in recent years. The fact that he came through a 6-inch hole on 4-pound-test line is almost a miracle. I won't be sticking my hand through a hole in the ice to grab a northern in the future, unless of course I think it is bigger than this one.

Scott Norton
Cicero, New York

North Wind

How many times have we heard the familiar adage, "When the wind is from the north, wise fishermen don't go forth?" I've recited it myself more than once, while on the water, getting a firsthand lesson in fishing futility. However, when one is fishing for a week up north for walleye and the only alternative is to sit in the cabin, wind from any direction isn't going to be a deterrent.

An urgent "Get the net!" request from my father broke the silence of that late August evening. An absolute silence—save for the wind blowing across the lake creating a "walleye" ripple—that allowed the sound of a low passing loon's wing strokes to filter down to our ears.

Variations of that request were repeated often that particular evening. A quick glance at the 4-foot-long ultralight rods held in my father's or mother's hands informed me if a net was needed. Hearing his reel's drag pay out line grudgingly was a good indication that it truly was.

My parents (Zig and Ann) and I were enjoying the sixth evening of 8 days on Onaping Lake, a deep, tannic-stained "tea-colored" lake located an hour-and-a-half's drive northwest of Sudbury, Ontario.

When the road literally ends at the government launch, another 23 miles by fully loaded boats are navigated to reach the remote camp. A very full boat—carrying all of our gear, food, gas and bait. The launch wouldn't be seen again until the end of our vacation.

The slow ride to camp allowed for a transition period of sorts—to unwind from the 6-hour drive and start taking in the scenery; as loons serenaded us along the way with their shrill welcome calls.

The rugged shoreline, while green and very beautiful, is of the type that after "one" picture there is simply no need to take anymore. Evergreens and white birch, of various windblown shapes and sizes, boulders and rock make up the vast majority of it. Still, that didn't stop us from exposing many rolls of film of favorite fishing holes, the fish that came from them and of our surroundings at any given time.

For 17 years, Onaping Lake has been my annual fishing vacation destination. For the past 2, my parents have been my guests and fishing partners. Walleye, northern pike and smallmouth bass are all available

quarry. During the week, the largest walleye caught exceeds 4 pounds. It isn't only for the solitude and fishing that we have traveled here, but also to renew old friendships with the owners and neighbors of the camp.

Good fishing was enjoyed each of the previous days and this day was no exception. In 20 minutes we would be pulling up anchors, as the sun had already ducked behind the evergreens and was continuing its trek toward the horizon. We looked forward to returning to the warmth of the cabin, quite satisfied with the day's fishing. There were fish to be cleaned and hot tea and hobo sandwiches on the menu.

Anchored in 18 feet of water from the bow and stern in a narrow channel, we intercepted walleye throughout the evening as they made their way from the deep bays into the shallows to feed. The Lund Pro-V 1660 provided us with a very comfortable fishing platform. Having caught-and-released, or kept walleye as the need arose for a shore lunch, we knew the routine and were each alone in our thoughts.

From time to time, my father mentioned what he had heard about the fishing not being very good in a north wind. I reminded him of that every time another bronze-colored walleye or bass came on board.

Now, seated in the bow, I started to concentrate on my fishing, while simultaneously scanning the vast amount of water and shoreline looking for any signs of wildlife. Over the years, I've had the fortune and privilege of observing moose, lynx, bear, beaver and mink in the water crossing the channels and bays.

It was shortly after that, the excited call for the net drifted forward from the stern. Swiveling around on the pedestal seat, I heard the reel's drag paying out line before seeing my father's arced rod. The rod tip was pointing straight down and pulsating under a heavy, moving weight. Dad was still seated, trying to keep the rod at a reasonable angle while the yet-to-be-identified and powerful fish was doing all it could to pull the rod from Dad's grasp.

In the excitement of the moment he had started to reel as fast as possible. The strength of the fish persuaded him to change tactics and just hang on. With net in hand and at the ready we all settled down for the ensuing battle.

Catching a glimpse of its large, reflective eyes as it broke the surface of the black water for the first time in the waning daylight left no doubt that it was indeed a walleye: the largest I had ever seen on this lake and it certainly wasn't ready to be netted.

A whirlpool-like swirl, dripping eyeglasses and a wet cold face were all that remained of the brief sighting. Thrusting its tail, it propelled itself back toward the dark, snag-laden floor of the channel in search of freedom—again distorting the rod and stripping the just-recovered line as it made its way. Despite the strength for two more similar attempts the hook remained firmly set in its lower jaw.

The "tug-of-war" ended 6 long minutes after it had begun when the lunker was scooped up into the awaiting net and hoisted aboard. It wasn't until the walleye was lying on the blue-carpeted floor that my parents saw the true size of what my father had caught and what I had known from the beginning.

My mother, who had unsuccessfully tried to avoid the camera all week, was now ready for photographs. Her wish had been that she would be the one to catch a trophy fish, but this would do for now. After all, there were two fishing days remaining.

Quickly deciding that this walleye would be mounted, we took many photographs before its coloring changed or faded. Many close-ups of the fish itself were taken to capture the true "northern waters" walleye coloring (black, gold and bronze) to help the taxidermist re-create the exact scheme.

Back at camp, by lantern light, the needle of the scale rested squarely on the 11-pound mark as we measured 29 inches of walleye. It was kept alive off of the end of the dock and transported home in the live well wrapped in a beach towel encased in ice.

It was a very memorable fishing trip for all of us. My father, who had celebrated his seventieth birthday earlier in the week, had caught a priceless birthday present. We can recall that evening vividly whenever we pass the mounted walleye, whom we've aptly nicknamed "North Wind."

John Zilgme
North Tonawanda, New York

My Biggest Thrill

For years my dad had been going up north with his buddies for a week of fishing in a remote area of Kipew Lake in Quebec. When I turned 12 he decided I was ready for my first adventure up there.

It was very exciting for me of course, and the beauty of that area will always be in my memories. The final leg of our trip we had to load all the gear into a boat and travel about 7 miles to reach our camp on a small island.

My biggest thrill came about the third day out. We had been bottom fishing for lake trout all morning in a small bay. This morning hadn't produced as well as some others, so my dad suggested that we head over closer to shore and make a few casts before we go in for lunch.

My line had been rigged with two hooks and a sinker at the bottom, so I took off the sinker and the bottom hook and tied on my favorite floating plug. I guess I was just being lazy leaving the top hook on, but decided to squeeze some split shot onto the shank of the hook. This would give me more weight to cast farther.

My first cast hit the water and there was a huge splash. A big old northern pike had been awakened. My heart was pounding as I fought to gain line whenever he relaxed. My dad was ready with the net as I finally got him up to the side of the boat. I just wish I could have seen our faces as he came to the surface and seconds later my favorite plug popped up. My lure was lying there, but I still had this lunker. He had hit that little top hook with the squeeze-on sinker.

Dad netted him for me and we both sat down and had a good laugh. In fact, to this day it is still one of the favorite stories shared by our group of fishing friends.

Rick Schreckengost
Submitted for my father by:
Darren Schreckengost
Cheektowaga, New York

Bye-Bye Walleye!

I am sending you a tale about an experience I had on Lake Mclintok in Plevna, Ontario, Canada, while on vacation for a week of walleye and bass fishing.

I went out one day to my favorite "honey hole." I fished with 8-pound Garcia Royal Bonnyl Line and Lindy Rig with ¼-ounce Lindy slip sinker and a #6 thin wire Mustad Aberdeen Hook with a nightcrawler. I caught a 9-inch smallmouth bass, and I had to cut the line to be able to release it alive.

The next day, I took my son-in-law out to the same spot and got a bite right away and, as I reeled in, something real big hit my line again. I told my son-in-law, "Hold the net ready in the water against the boat and when I bring it up, slip the net under the fish and lift it into the boat." He was so excited that he bumped the fish under its neck, and it just opened its mouth and spit my 9-inch bass out and said bye-bye! The bass still had my Mustad #6 hook in its mouth from the day before. It was real live, so I just cut the line and released it again with both hooks in its mouth. I was real happy to see it swim away again, after its 2-day ordeal. The fish was a real big walleye and had to be at least 10 pounds. I caught and lost several large walleye and bass in this

lake in my 15 years of fishing trips up there. I'll be 84 in June and may not be able to go up there to catch and lose a big one again.

Joseph Kalo
Elyria, Ohio

Never Give Up

Being a retired law enforcement officer, I have always believed that you should respect your quarry, and protect the habitat and the resources that God created for all of us. Think about when the disciples (some were fishermen) couldn't get any fish. The Lord told them where to cast their nets. If you remember, the boat began to sink from fish.

I have known some people for years who never caught a muskie of any size. With catch-and-release and stocking programs, this should improve.

Bob, the father of one of my best friends, who has since passed away, made a statement to me a few years back, "You have so much luck in catching muskies, I believe that if you fell out of your boat, a bunch of them would swim up and probably help you back into the boat."

No matter how tough conditions get, you can't give

up. I never said muskie hunting is easy. A good friend of mine caught his first legal with me on his first trip on his first cast. It took him 9 years after that to catch his second legal. He was thinking about giving up muskie fishing, as I was the one who talked him into spending all his money on fishing equipment. Well, he has changed his mind for the best again. This past year, he kicked butt and caught a 48½-incher, 30 pounds, and released it.

Enough said. I have plenty of stories I have written about my fishing partner. The best was 17 fish in the boat, follows or lost in one day during the fall of 1994. Another perfect day.

A. Jim Heffner
Brodhead, Wisconsin

Talk About Luck

While fishing in Casey's Dock Tournament on August 27, 2000, the team of Tim Boice, George Boice and Mike Newmen were out fishing for bass when Mike hooks one about 12 inches. While reeling him a muskellunge grabs the bass and runs just about all of his line off the reel. After chasing and battling this fish for 10 or 15 minutes, we finally got a net on him. Later at weigh-in, the 53-inch muskie tipped the scales at 39 pounds, 4 ounces. With this trophy, and 15 bass in all, we won the contest with 110 points. All these men belong to the George Washington Fishing & Camping Club.

P.S. Eight-pound test and a #8 hook took this lunker muskie.

George Boice
Buffalo, New York

One for the Wall

Every June a group of guys take a fishing trip to Ontario, Canada. In June of 1998 I happened to go along. On our 14-hour journey to Ontario, the other guys who had gone the year before were talking about a lake they had found. We normally fish at Lount Lake Outpost Camp on the English River.

The guys were looking at a map of the area and found Moose Lake. The only way to get to this lake was to park the boat on shore and portage to it. They were talking about the size of the northern pike in this lake. It was basically a trophy lake. On Tuesday, Danny, Rudy, Jeff and I decided to make the trip to Moose Lake and give it a try.

We gathered up a minimal amount of tackle and supplies we would need to fish there. We parked our boat and grabbed our gear. After about 45 minutes of walking through forests and stepping over fallen trees and avoiding various holes in the ground, we made it to our destination. At the lake were two aluminum boats and only one motor. There also was twine that we used to tie the boats together. We all got situated and started our day of fishing, Danny and Rudy in the first boat, Jeff and I in the boat behind them. It wasn't long before Jeff and I realized that our boat had a slight leak coming from one of the rivet holes.

We took turns every 10 minutes to bail the water. After about half an hour, the first northern pike was caught. Pretty soon everyone was catching fish except for me. I started out using a Luhr-Jensen Loco and then switched to a gold Johnson's Silver Minnow. Still no bites. I then switched to a floating diving Rapala which Jeff was using, and catching fish. Still nothing. By this time I was getting a little aggravated.

After about 2 hours of switching lures with no luck, I was ready to go back. I had on a silver Loco and was just casting to try and get something. I didn't make this journey for nothing. As Danny was motoring to a different location, I cast out my lure. I got snagged on something. I told Danny to stop so I could try to free my lure. I started pulling on my rod and whatever I was snagged on was coming toward the boat. As it got closer my adrenaline kicked in when I saw it was a huge pike. Then the fun began.

The pike took off toward the bottom of the lake, taking line off my reel. The northern slowed down a bit so I reeled it back up to the boat and it took off again. I played with this fish for what seemed like an eternity. Finally the northern tired out and I was able to bring it to the side of the boat one last time. Jeff helped me land this monster. This was the biggest fish that I have ever caught. It was a 16-pound, 36-inch northern pike. This made me forget about the 2 hours of terrible fishing. I think I had a big smile on my face the rest of the week.

That one fish made my entire trip wonderful. The fish is now hanging on my wall with the "retired" lure I used to catch it in its mouth. Everytime I look at it I think back to how great a time I had.

Charles M. Simon
Hoffman Estates, Illinois

Is Fishing for the Birds?

Living in Manitoba, nothing beats fishing in late September on the Winnipeg River when the greenbacks (pickerel) are running. When you get to go once and experience this, you want to go every chance you get. It was in late September that a friend and I planned a Friday morning fishing trip to Fine Falls, Manitoba. He phoned me Thursday night and told me his boat was ready to go, so we made our plans.

As I was getting my gear ready the next morning at 5:00 a.m., I received the dreaded phone call from my friend, saying he had to work and we were not going. Because I was excited and ready to go, I decided to go by myself anyway and fish from shore.

I left Winnipeg and got to Pine Falls in a little over an hour. I stopped at the bait shop and bought two tubs of minnows for bait. I drove to the boat launch where you could fish from the riverbank. I parked my truck at the bottom of the rocks and climbed up to fish. I began fishing and was using pickerel rigs with minnows. After about 45 minutes, I caught a nice 2½-pound pickerel. I put it on my stringer and baited my line again. I left the lid off the tub of minnows and put my rod in a rod holder. I decided to go to my truck to get my thermos of coffee and lunch. When I returned, I noticed I had company. A seagull had decided to make my tub of minnows his lunch. He had his head in the tub and was eating away. I ran after him, but he didn't really go too far. He just hung around a while and didn't seem too shy. I closed the tub of minnows and kept it beside me.

After about 20 minutes, I caught another pickerel. I laid my rod down and took the fish off the bottom hook of the pickerel rig. I then turned around to put my fish on the stringer.

When I turned around to get my rod, I saw my seagull friend was eating the remaining minnow from the top hook of my pickerel rig. I immediately yelled and walked toward him. I startled him and he started to run away, but the hook was stuck in his beak. As he was dragging my rod away, he was shaking his head trying to free the hook. I started to panic because this was a brand-new Shimano rod and reel I had purchased for the fishing season.

As the seagull started to fly toward the river, my rod was bouncing off the rocks. In a last effort to get it back I chased the seagull and dove at my rod, only to helplessly see it bounce out of reach and fall over the riverbank. As I lay there on the rocks, I saw the rod floating and slowly starting to sink into the river. The seagull was in the water furiously shaking his head to free the hook. I shared concern for both the seagull and my beloved rod.

As I considered jumping in to retrieve my rod, the seagull finally freed itself and then we both watched as my rod disappeared forever. I fished for another few hours with my spare rod, but couldn't stop pouting, so I decided to call it a day. As I was leaving, I noticed the seagull had stuck around. Admitting defeat, I threw him the rest of my bait and left. You know my tip:

• Not only do fish like minnows; so do seagulls, so always keep a lid on your bait.

Dan Robinson
Winnipeg, Manitoba, Canada

Lure Retrieval

Years ago I took a young, husky real estate salesman on a wilderness trip in northwest Ontario. He said that he could get tackle and I took him at his word. When he unpacked it, I was awed. I hadn't seen a jointed steel rod with a single-action winch-type reel for years, but he borrowed it.

I couldn't bear to give him any real good lure, because I knew he would lose it on the first good-sized fish he managed to hook. So I dug out the oldest, worst Dardevle I could find and hooked it on his rod. Sure enough, he hooked a lunker northern pike. Well, the battle resulted in a king-sized backlash, skinned, bloody knuckles, and loss of a worthless lure.

After about 15 minutes of first aid, getting the backlash cleared and consultation, I sneaked back to the spot, cast and hooked a 16½-pound northern pike. When it was boated, it had the old Dardevle in its mouth, my hook hooked through the hook on the old Dardevle.

I turned to the fisherman and said, "I'll tie this on again, but try not to lose it again. I can't always retrieve them." And the new fisherman believed it!!

Shows how vicious the big old northerns are in remote lakes.

Howard Gaston
Naples, Florida

Joyce's Big Catch

It started out on one of those nice Sunday afternoons when I "convinced" my wife, Joyce, to go with me fishing. We got our fishing gear together and put it in our small motor home. With food, bait and rods loaded, we headed for our local lake.

We found a nice spot on the bank to try our luck. We baited our crappie rigs with worms that I had dug earlier and began our wait. The afternoon was enjoyable, but the fish were not very interested in being caught (but we were still having fun).

Dusk was setting in quickly, so I decided to get the lantern. While I was in the motor home, Joyce got a bite. She thought she missed it, so she waited for the next tug. When it came, she knew she had a big fish on. She started to yell at me to come and help, but I was still in the motor home and I did not hear her. As she fought the fish, she got more excited and started to scream for me to get there. When I finally came out and heard her, I quickly ran down to help Joyce in her struggle to land the fish.

All the yelling created quite a stir on the lake. People came to investigate what all the excitement was about. Everyone watching, including me, was happy when Joyce landed her 10-pound, 8-ounce walleye, which is a Master Angler Award Fish in Nebraska.

This just goes to show you that it does not take fancy equipment or skill to catch the big one!

Glen Rodick
Bancroft, Nebraska

Easier Casting

If the rod and reel you are using is not working the best, dunk the reel in the water to clean and lubricate the line. You will find that the line casts easier and farther.

Glen Rodick
Bancroft, Nebraska

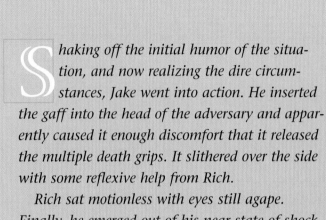

*S*haking off the initial humor of the situation, and now realizing the dire circumstances, Jake went into action. He inserted the gaff into the head of the adversary and apparently caused it enough discomfort that it released the multiple death grips. It slithered over the side with some reflexive help from Rich.

Rich sat motionless with eyes still agape. Finally, he emerged out of his near state of shock to collect himself. "Jake, he almost got me!"

—From "A 'Fish' Tale"

Saltwater Excitement

A Whale of a Tale

From muddy bayous to lakes and rivers, the waters of Louisiana offer fun, excitement and surprise. Recently I was invited on my first offshore fishing excursion near Grand Chenier. A party of six cut through the choppy Gulf Coast waters aboard a 25-foot craft, the FISHTALE. Three-foot swells rocked the vessel as we hooked onto one of the many oil platforms rising out of the waves.

Cigar minnows were the bait of choice. Large metal hooks were poked through their bulging, black eyeballs, then back through their smooth, shiny torsos, and finally plunked overboard plummeting through depths of darkness at the ends of lead-weighted lines. Who knew what might be awaiting these tempting tidbits!

Once past the spade fish, it wasn't long before I felt a tug. My heart jumped and I immediately shifted into a "fright-flight" mode. My drag was singing. The line was leaving its nice, neat spool in a whir of retreat! Do I reel, or do I run? Whatever had sampled my savory lure made the decision for me. It had decided not to pursue the tasty morsel—but too late! The fishy was mine. I planted the padded end of the pole under my right arm and began to reel with all I could muster.

"Lift the tip of your rod. Keep the line tight. Set your hook. Don't let it near the rig. Keep it away from the motors." Instructions were flying left and right. I kept reeling and it kept unreeling all that I had reclaimed. My mind was spinning. Visions of a majestic marlin or a vicious shark filled my fantasies! What was hooked at the end of my rod?

"Please, Lord." I was praying. This was kinda exciting, kinda scary, kinda fun and kinda exasperating all at the the same time. The mystery catch had emerged within sight of the "spectators." Shouts went out. It's a KING! A 5-foot king mackerel was gaffed and pulled aboard with the help of several crew members. Next, red snapper and, finally, several sharks were loaded into the ice chest before our trip was complete. What a day!

The seagulls had visited to beg and see what we had to share. Porpoises had been seen playing in the surf. The winds and waters had allowed our fishing party a day without harm or havoc. The dramamine had worked; and our ice chest was full of the finest assortment our Gulf had to offer. What more could we ask for?

As the mooring hook was disengaged from the rig, we all took one last look around, scanning the horizon. In the distance, a white mist arose, followed by a dark hump. We thought, just another porpoise, perhaps. But, to our grand surprise—an ending of another sort! The tail of a whale waved us farewell, as we cut 'cross the waters of the Gulf off the coast of Grand Chenier. My tip is easy:

• Besides the customary fishing tackle: rods, lures, bait, etc.—don't forget your camera!

Jane Prentice
Jonesville, Louisiana

Go Light for Big Sharks

Though heavy tackle would seem necessary to tackle sharks, truth is that you'll have more fun with light big-game tackle.

Because sharks are usually caught in open-water situations, an angler who takes his time playing his quarry can get by with 20- to 30-pound-class tackle. Larger sharks may require heavier tackle—makos, for example, 50-pound gear; whites, tigers and giant makos, 80—but using heavier gear than is necessary really takes away from the fun of the fight.

No matter how light you go, however, respect the sharp teeth that contribute to the fierce mystique that sharks evoke. Larger sharks, especially, require the use of 15 feet of single-strand wire in sizes 12 to 15. To avoid kinks or twists, however, you may wish to use heavy monofilament as the top of your leader, then tie on a swivel to which you should connect a few feet of the wire at the terminal end.

Glenn Sapir
Shrub Oak, New York

Getting Bunkers for Blues

Successfully catching bait can be a key to fishing success, and when it comes to catching bluefish, striped bass and a variety of other saltwater sportfish, anglers should know how to get their own menhaden, a particularly attractive bait.

These oily herring, better known as mossbunkers or just bunkers, are big enough to make freshwater anglers embarrassed about going after 8-inch trout. Get one of these bunkers on your line, especially when foul-hooked, and anglers with light tackle are in for a tussle. They make bait-catching fun.

Finding the bunkers is the real challenge. Having friends out on the water, with their radios on, makes locating the bait easier, as their reports can guide you to schools. When you are on your own, however, depend on your eyes. Look for "nervous" water: that is, a change in the surface from the water around it. That change can range from slight ripples to obvious splashes, where the bait are surfacing, likely being chased by blues, stripers or other predators.

A weighted treble snagging hook, popular, where legal, with Great Lakes salmon fishermen who foul-hook the would-be spawners, is the ticket. Cast into this nervous water, let the hook sink a few feet below the surface, then continually make sharp yanks with your rod, as if you were setting the hook into a monstrous fish. Each time you yank, reel in the newly created slack line. If the fish are there, you will likely connect with a bunker.

Your efforts will be rewarded not only with productive baitfish, but also with a lot of fun-filled fishing action while collecting your bait.

Glenn Sapir
Shrub Oak, New York

A "Fish" Tale

(This is a true story as related to member Dan Archuleta)

It was a beautiful day off the coast of Shelter Cove, northern California. The sea was nearly calm and the bottom fishing was great for blues, snapper and lingcod.

Retired firefighters "Jake" McKinnon and Rich Rowe were in the process of cranking up varieties of delicious table fare into Jake's 16-foot aluminum boat. Jake was contemplating the long run back to harbor, the filleting chores and the drive to Sparks, Nevada. Suddenly, Rich bellowed, "Fish on! Fish on! Feels like a big one. Feels like a lotta weight!" Jake readied himself with the gaff and peered intently over the side into the depths. Rich cranked, took line, adjusted drag and

cranked some more. Rich exclaimed, "He's coming up! He's coming up!" Jake became more intense and at the same time wondered how Rich could tell what gender the fish was.

Jake was focused on the blue-green water below the boat, hoping to catch the first flash of color as the fish approached. It crossed Rich's mind several times as he took line and lifted, that this fish didn't pump the rod as was usual. He kept at it, feeling the strain on his aging muscles, his eyes now approaching the size of silver dollars.

"Look at that!"

Just below the small boat an

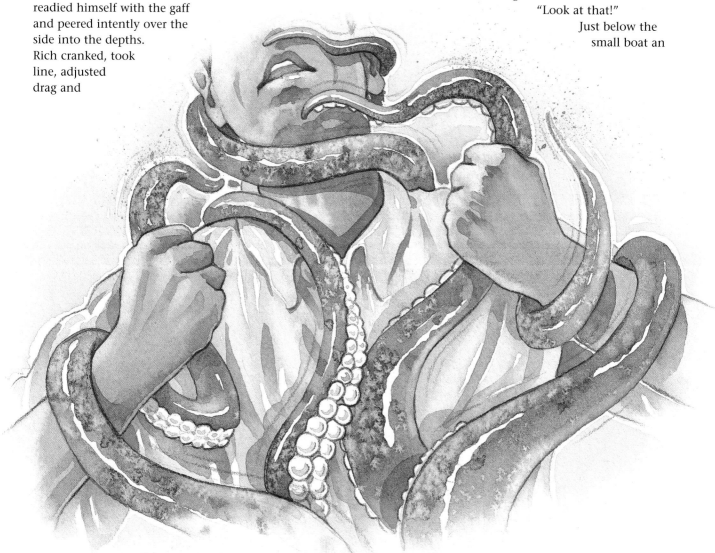

orange-green apparition began to take shape, flaying to and fro in desperate combat with the heavy leader. Rich was seated well back in the seat and could not see what Jake had. Now Jake's facial expression became more serious, yet with a slight smile, and eyes gleaming. Loudly Jake announced, "I understand octopus is great eating!" The beast was now close enough to the surface for Rich to see. He yelled, "Cut it loose, cut it loose!" Undaunted, and with mission in mind, Jake thrust the gaff into the huge squirming mess, and in the same motion, using his 200-plus weight, had it in the boat. WRONG!

In a heartbeat, two or three tentacles were draped over the gunnel and attached firmly to the hull. The others were encoiled around Rich's arms, neck and face! He had made the mistake of leaning near the creature to dislodge the hook.

Initially, Jake giggled slightly at Rich's predicament, somewhat seeming to enjoy the sight of the mess of fish and friend. Rich would use all his strength to tear a tentacle away from his face and throat. As quickly, another would replace the one removed. Disc shaped red welts began to appear on his face and neck. Now the situation was not in the least bit funny! Rich was losing the battle.

Shaking off the initial humor of the situation, and now realizing the dire circumstances, Jake went into action. He inserted the gaff into the head of the adversary and apparently caused it enough discomfort that it released the multiple death grips. It slithered over the side with some reflexive help from Rich.

Rich sat motionless with eyes still agape. Finally, he emerged out of his near state of shock to collect himself. "Jake, he almost got me!" Jake still wondered how Rich could tell the critter was a male. He opened a cold one and leaned back, giggling mischievously. In a few moments the giggle disappeared.

For suddenly, as he was watching Rich "get it together," a tentacle whipped over the bow of the boat near Rich's position, then another. Rich almost messed himself. "This time it's going to be different," cracked Jake. He grabbed his ready fillet knife, moved quickly to the front of the boat as Rich retreated. Jake attacked steadfastly and severed each tentacle as it appeared with surgeonlike perfection. Finally, what was left of the critter drifted off into the depths of the Pacific, sans some edibles left behind.

Jake and Rich still fish the same area from time to time. When this story is told over and over in local water holes, it continues to produce gut-busting hilarity and some spitting and spilling of suds. A funny adventure that could have turned out tragic. My tip? It's obvious:

• When fishing ocean waters and hooking a giant squid (octopus), do not haul it into your small boat.

Dan Archuleta
Sparks, Nevada

More Whale Tales

My first ever California yellowtail came last July near northern Baja's Coronado Islands. The first of two fish for my day hit a live sardine and, as I fought the fish, a crew member, unhappy with my tight drag setting, loosened it up, more to his liking. I assumed his quick adjustment was sound and so kept it there. Late in the day, another fish struck a sardine and we locked into a seesaw stalemate.

Reluctantly, but wishing to decide the battle, I retightened my drag and within 5 minutes the tail was up to gaff. The 25-minute ordeal, however, took its toll on my Trilene knot because even before the fish hit the deck, the knot slipped out, leaving a corkscrew tag end and 1/0 hook in the fish's lip. Talk about too close for comfort!

Both were trophy-class yellowtail on 17-pound Vanish, Penn number 140 Squidder reel and Sabre Rod.

Case in point ... scale-test your drag beforehand for accuracy and familiarity, which I plan to do on future trips!

Daniel G. Flores
Montclair, California

The "Baby" Blue Marlin

My wife and I have traveled to Mexico many times. We have fished the Pacific Ocean side for tuna and sailfish with good success. This fishing trip would be our first on the Caribbean side.

The day before our trip we toured the ruins of Chichén Itzá, which is a large Mayan pyramid in Yucatán Province. It was a wonderful and tiring tour, but we had booked a trip out of Puerto Aventuras the next morning with Capt. Ric's Adventures. Our tour bus from Chichén Itzá did not arrive home until 8:00 p.m. that night. It was hard to get up so early the next morning, then get in a cab for a 1-hour ride to Puerto Aventuras from our hotel near Playa Del Carmen.

Our captain told us that the blue marlin were biting. The day before, one had been boated. Our fishing trip in June coincided with peak blue marlin season. The boat was a 23-foot Seacraft with a 225-hp Evinrude. Boats down here in Mexico are simple in comparison to the larger boats in the States. We chose a 4-hour trip. Little did we know that the fight with a marlin would take up all of those 4 hours.

The ride out to the fishing grounds was short, just 1 mile. Unfortunately, the seas were rough, about 4 feet. Accustomed to the calmer Pacific Ocean side, both of us got seasick. My dinner from the previous night wound up in the ocean. Afterward, both of us napped in the boat's cabin. I was awakened by the mate after about ½ hour of trolling.

He said, "Blue marlin!" He handed me the rod, as he had already hooked the fish. As the marlin greyhounded across the water, the mate said, "The marlin does not like it." The fight evolved into a series of runs after which I would pump and reel. At times the fish was in front of the boat and the captain would follow. I sometimes had to reel like mad to keep the line tight. Little did I know that this was the "fun part" of the fight. Our boat had no chair, only a cooler for a fighting chair, and my only other equipment besides the rod and reel was a rod belt to keep the fishing rod from digging into my waist.

I had the marlin close to the boat several times, but just as the mate was about to grab the leader for the release, the fish would make another run, taking all of the line I had gained. The fish decided to go deep and the fight wore on. As the captain decided to back down on the fish, water came over the transom and I took a shower. Good thing I had my bathing suit on. Water filled the back of the boat, but the outboard kept running. The fish would not budge from the depths and any attempt to pump and reel would be met by the line slipping out anyway. There was not much energy left in me after 1½ hours of pumping and reeling. My wife started to complain that I was too slow in reeling in the Marlin and wanted the line to be cut. I said "No way!" and offered her the fishing rod. She declined, saying the fish was my problem, so I finally gave the rod to the mate and he worked the fish for an hour trying to get it to the surface. The fish would not budge.

Now it was the captain's turn to pump and reel. He had better luck by holding his thumb on the reel as he would pump the fish to prevent the line from slipping. The captain told us that the fish had died sometime during the fight and would have to be hand-lined to the surface. This helped some. After about 1 hour of hand lining and pumping and reeling, the fish finally surfaced.

It was dead, of course, and there was no point in releasing it. The captain and the mate struggled to get the 160-pound marlin in the boat and finally made it after the boat dipped into an oncoming wave enough to slide the marlin in. The fish was also fouled around the line, which would explain the long fight. Sometime during the fight, the fish had wrapped the line around one of his forward fins. The captain and the mate congratulated me, and my wife took pictures. It was sad that the fish died, but here in Mexico nothing is wasted. The fish would be divided between us and the crew.

As far as marlin go, this was a baby. Marlin get much bigger, up to 1500 pounds. In fact, a huge brute of a marlin battled a fisherman off of the island of Cozumel for 11 hours before breaking the line. Imagine the heartbreak of that fisherman!

Back at the dock, a crowd gathered together to see the fish. We were late getting back as our trip took longer than 4 hours. The party waiting for their afternoon 4-hour trip was impressed by the fish and asked me if they would catch one. I told them they would get something. There are other gamefish, such as sailfish, white marlin, dorado, tuna, sierra mackerel and wahoo. They actually told me that they wanted something smaller as they were a young couple and didn't want to fight a fish for 3½ hours. After the fish was cleaned, divided and the captain and mate tipped, we got our taxi ride home. Our cab driver, after hearing about our trip, said fighting a marlin was like fighting a bull. My wife's Mexican relatives enjoyed eating our marlin when we traveled to Mexico City for the rest of our vacation.

If I have any tips for anyone fishing for marlin, it would be to let the mate hook the fish. This is tricky for a beginner and should only be attempted if there are a lot of fish around and there is a patient teacher who speaks good English. You do not want to blow your only chance at a marlin, because some days only one fish will be caught. Billfish slash at the bait and then return to eat it. Sometimes the fish just follows the bait without attacking. The line is free-spooled until the fish starts to run with the bait. Once this happens, the reel is put in gear to the strike position and the hook is set.

To set the hook properly, all the slack must be reeled in and then the angler has to rear back on the rod two or three times to set the hook. Usually the captain guns the motor to help set the hook. Once the fight is underway, the mate will instruct you on proper pumping and reeling technique. The rod is brought toward you and then lowered slowly. Reel in line as the rod is lowered.

Do not rest, as the fish rests when you do. Try to end the fight quickly, as the fish will go deep if the fight lasts too long. This is not always easy to do and requires someone in good shape, especially if the fight lasts for 11 hours. Throughout the fight the drag will have to be readjusted and the line level winded. Follow all instructions of the mate.

Best time to try for a blue marlin off of Cancún, Isla Mujeres, and the Mexican Riviera down to Akumel is June and July. Fish run about 120 to 160 pounds, but can be much bigger. Expect seas to be 3 to 4 feet, somewhat rougher than the Pacific Ocean on average. Bring some sea sickness pills. Good luck and tight lines.

Richard P. Gunion
Washington, D.C.

Catching Marlin, Plane and Simple

Marlin are truly big-game fish, and getting them to the boat, once they are hooked, is a tremendous challenge. They fight like they are educated, so I got educated myself, attending a seminar on fighting the bluewater giants. I learned about "planing," a helpful technique when the big fish are hanging deep and can't be budged. It's a process that when repeated may very well get the marlin to the surface, or at least, stimulate a run.

1. Lessen your reel's drag a little, then slowly advance the boat for 100 feet.

2. Return the drag to its previous setting, then back throttle about 50 feet while the angler retrieves the slack line.

3. Repeat the process, for you are shortening the distance between you and the fish, moving it to the surface, with each repetition.

By repeating this planing technique, you will force fish to drop their "won't budge" tactics.

Glenn Sapir
Shrub Oak, New York

Doc and the Bucket

My fishing partner and I were fishing in south Louisiana near Grand Isle, in a saltwater bay near the Gulf of Mexico. We had fished the same spot in the morning, and caught a nice mess of speckled trout (spotted sea bass) so we returned in the afternoon to catch more.

As soon as we arrived and began fishing my partner caught three nice trout in a row. We were fishing out of a large aluminum flat boat with a center console. I was in the back and he was in the front.

A couple of weeks before, I had purchased several new plastic fishing baits at a Sportsmen's Show and decided that I would try one of these new lures. It was a large reddish plastic shrimp. On the first cast, a large fish smashed my line and I set the hook. Line stripped off and the battle began. My partner, Doc, stood behind me as we tried to figure out what I had hooked. After about 25 minutes of drag pulling and reeling the fish broke the surface about 25 yards off the stern of the boat. It was a huge red drum. I told Doc to get ready with the net because I wanted to land the fish and get its measurement and release it.

Just about the time the fish seemed ready to land I said, "Doc, land it on the right side of the boat near the front so I can keep the line out of the prop—ready!" As I tried to steer the fish to the right side, I did not see Doc. I looked behind the console and he was sitting on a 5-gallon plastic bucket—pants down, with a roll of toilet paper in his hand! I said, "Are you nuts? Get the net." He replied, "Nature called."

I let the fish swim for a couple of minutes and finally Doc netted the fish. It was 46 inches long and 34 pounds. I had lip-hooked the fish, so we removed the hook, put the fish back, and watched it swim away. I then started laughing and will never forget Doc and the bucket.

Mike Dwyer
New Orleans, Louisiana

What's it Called?

Red drum are obviously part of the drum family. Their name gives that away. In fact, they are the largest of the drums. Yet, red drum is not the name given to the fish everywhere.

The red drum ranges from Virginia down to Florida on the Atlantic Coast and from Texas to Florida on the Gulf Coast. Depending where it is caught, you might hear another handle for the species. Redfish is a common term; another is reds. Those terms are common along the Gulf. Channel bass is a term more popularly used along the southern Atlantic Coast.

The one name that doesn't change is its taxonomic name: *Sclanenops ocellatus*. They can be most easily identified by one or more black spots, called ocelli, which appear on their tail.

Glenn Sapir
Shrub Oak, New York

Thrill for a New Fisherman

This is a story about a country girl being exposed to shark fishing. When my wife Peg and I moved from Pennsylvania to Virginia, one of the first things we did was buy a boat. Not just any boat, but an old Pacemaker, 36 feet long. I spent as much time as I could on that old boat, but it seemed that Peg always had other things that needed to be done.

Finally, one day she had nothing to use for a reason not to come out on the boat with me. I used all the little tricks I had picked up to try to get her hooked up to a flounder or weakfish (trout), but it seemed they had all developed lockjaw. I was beginning to worry that I was going to lose a fishing partner before I even had one! That's when I remembered the spot that I had stumbled across while I was looking for "real" fish. It always had small shark there, and they always seemed to be hungry.

We moved to the spot and I cut up some of the crabs, used a small hook and caught a small croaker, which became our bait. In a very short time the sharks were there looking for a free meal. What a surprise! The free meal had a hook in it! We must have caught 15 or 20 of those 3-foot sharks before we quit, and we did keep a couple to try on the grill (and very tasty, too, I might add). The rest of them were released. From then on I had a new fishing partner and that has continued for 29 years now. Since then we have developed a system that works well for us.

Our system is to find a drop-off and anchor up current. We use cut bait (mostly trash fish) and fairly heavy gear, since most of the fish we catch are in the 6- to 12-foot range. We use fairly heavy sinkers (8-plus ounces) and since we know the depth of the drop-off, we tie a balloon to the line where the bait is just off the bottom. We drift the bait back to the edge of the drop-off and wait. Whenever one of the balloons either sinks or goes for a ride it's time to hang on! This system works well for us and has produced a lot of sharks for us in the last 29 years. Since the sharks are being fished fairly heavily, we now tag 100 percent of what we catch, and release almost all of them.

Capt. E. N. "Red" Lorish
Woodbine, New Jersey

The Giant Shadow of the Deep

One day in June, Jonathan (my nephew) and I decided to go fishing for some sharks. We left Caxambas Pass ramp on Marco Island at about 2 o'clock, hoping to be back at the dock by 6 before the ramp closed and locked us in for the night. First, we went around the island jigging for anything for bait, since I always like to use fresh bait. We caught a few jacks and time was kinda running out, since by that time it was about 5 p.m. I had not fished right out of the pass in a while so, what the heck, I thought, let's try it.

We went about a mile out of Caxambas Pass. The seas were nice and we anchored up on the tide line. The tide was going out and the current was not too bad. I put a live jack out behind the boat and free-lined with the current. I put out another half a jack on a different line on the bottom. Sure enough, about 15 minutes later the half jack starts going out really slowly. I tell Jonathan to grab the rod and jerk as hard as he can. The 50-pound line starts going out like it was nothing but dental floss, and the battle began. My Shimano Triton 15 TLD reel had plenty of line and, in thinking that, I noticed the fish was not slowing down. The reel had about a quarter spool left when I thought, "Time to pull up anchor and go after him." Good thing we did, because that fish, whatever it was, didn't slow down or speed up for a long time.

About 15 minutes into the fight, my nephew decided his back couldn't take anymore and handed the pole to me. The fish was going straight out from the pass. We were about 1½ miles out by then.

"Did we hook a submarine?"

We had to start the engine to follow and catch up to the fish every few minutes to gain a bit of line on it. By this time, we were about 45 minutes into this fight and hadn't seen the fish yet. I figured out we were about 2½ miles out, the ramp was going to close soon, it was getting dark, and this was the biggest fish I had ever hooked.

"Please God, let me see this thing and I promise I will release it."

About this time we were gaining on it by chasing it with the motor. Jonathan was at the wheel and suddenly I noticed I only had about 20 yards of line left. I went out on the front deck of my Hewes and fought as hard as I could. I looked down just under the boat and could barely see a huge shadow on the other end of my line. I estimated it to be about 10 to 12 feet long. All I could make out was a huge shadow. And once again, it dove back down to the depths of the bottom.

Now we were 50 minutes into the fight. Both of us had fought this fish for about 25 minutes each and all we saw was a shadow bigger than any other fish I ever caught.

I had this fish on the biggest rig on my boat, which usually brings in 7- to 8-foot lemon sharks in about 10 to 15 minutes, even when I'm playing with them. Both of us tired of fighting this fish, our backs killing us, I decided to horse him a little more. SNAP goes the line. Fifty-eight minutes into the fight. We never really saw what it was. The fight was over.

We were somewhat relieved, but mad we were never able to identify the giant fish. It was all over. After talking to a few guides from around the area and knowing what I know of the area, I believe it was a huge sawfish, bull shark or hammerhead of about 11 or 12 feet.

At the ramp, we found it had closed for the night. We had to call the police. We told the police we had had engine trouble and couldn't get back before the gate was locked. Of course, I could not tell him exactly why we didn't get back on time, thinking that the police officer would not consider a great fight a very good excuse to get locked out of the boat ramp. If only the officer knew that was the biggest fish I had ever fought and lost.

This is an event I will never forget, and I will be sure to go back again, after that monster from the deep. Always be prepared for the big one when you go out. You never know when a monster will get on your line.

I have pictures of us fighting this monster. Now that I think of it, I'll just go fishing tonight in the same place. I hope I don't get locked out of the boat ramp again—or do I?

John Brossard
Naples, Florida

A Little Help Here

Many of us learn to fish as kids, yet our high school and college years can take us away from fishing, as they did me. But however great the enthusiasm of rediscovery, don't forget the basics, like safety.

On a November 2-day trip out of Santa Barbara, California, our rockfish charter set up its first morning drift. I had chosen to throw a 4-ounce Crippled Herring lure with a Berkley Power Bait plastic tail laced on the long-shank Siwash hook.

Upon raising my third catch of the morning, I attempted to swing the four-pounder over the rail. It seemed to be well hooked and I had no fear of losing the fish; at which point, the hook let go. Under strain from the rod, with reel in gear, the lure launched into a perfect arc, fully embedding the large hook in my right forearm.

Luckily, the captain and charter master were just down the rail from me. Ever heard the line, "a little help"? Well, it works!

Thankfully, the seasoned skipper, Ron, was able to remove the hook with minimal damage. After a stiff drink and extended break, I was able to fish the remainder of the trip.

Please, in any emergency, remain calm and seek appropriate assistance. And, I definitely got a tetanus shot!

Daniel G. Flores
Montclair, California

Holy Mackerel— A Great Rig for Yellowtail

Yellowtail are a great gamefish, but an angler needs all the help he can get to hook into these aquatic bulldogs. A favorite yellowtail rig described by outdoor writer Blad Evanoff works great for fishing live mackerel as bait. Here's his advice:

Thread from 2 to 6 sliding sinkers onto your line, then tie on a barrel swivel to serve as a sinker stop. To the terminal end of the swivel, tie on a 4-foot leader and an 8/0 or 9/0 hook. Hook the live mackerel through both lips, from bottom to top, exposing the hook point. This rig is effective for bottom fishing.

Glenn Sapir
Shrub Oak, New York

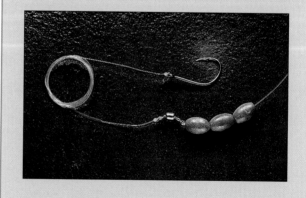

The Creature in Oaks Creek

It was an unusually calm morning as I launched my small boat at the state park ramp in Murrells Inlet. I wanted to catch a mess of crabs as a special treat for my guests. The best area to accomplish this, in my estimation, is Oaks Creek. There wasn't another boat on the water, so I was able to hear every sound made by the area wildlife. It was beautiful to be so alone and in harmony with nature.

As I baited my first crab pot, I could literally see hundreds of large mullet jumping in the creek. After all the pots were baited and in place, maybe I could catch some by throwing a shrimp net that luckily was stowed aboard. As I moved the craft to the next location, I glanced back to make sure that the first pot marker buoy was out of the channel. Looking back, I saw what appeared to be a human head bob out of the water near my marker buoy. It submerged again before I could positively identify it. Placing the rest of the crab pots in the water, I saw the head come to the surface, this time at a greater distance than before, and I still could not identify it.

After all the crab pots were in my chosen locations, I headed the boat toward an area teeming with mullet. On the very first cast of the shrimp net I pulled up two mullet weighing in excess of 2 pounds each. That would be enough for us. Because I live close to the sea, I don't take any fish over the amount that I am able to use immediately. My next casts were for live bait for the two rods that I took along to occupy some of the time while out on the water. One bait bucket was filled with live shrimp and the other was filled with juvenile pinfish.

I traveled up the creek in search of an anchorage suitable for both crabbing and fishing. I dropped six lines into the water, baited with chicken necks and held in place with 3-ounce bank sinkers, hoping to pick up a few additional crabs to supplement the crabs that invariably would be captured in the pots. Then one rod was baited with live shrimp. It must seem funny to most people that anyone would use shrimp for bait instead of eating them. Let me assure you that they do get eaten, but the shrimp are so abundant in our waters that using them for bait is a common practice. And besides, what do you think is the food most of the fish here prefer? The other rod was baited with the small pinfish.

The first crab line that I pulled up was empty. What I am trying to say is that it really was empty. The bait and the 3-ounce sinker were completely gone! I thought that something on the bottom must have cut the line above the setup. To my amazement, the other crab lines suffered a similar fate. No bait or sinker! I was starting to get very worried now. I could not comprehend any of the weird occurrences that had happened up until now. Every time I reeled a line in on one of the rods, the bait was gone except for one occasion when I managed to hook a 2-pound stingray. Toward the end of the day I became more comfortable because other boats were anchored within view. Finally a slight tap on one of the rods signaled it was time to set the hook. I fought a huge submarine creature for almost an hour before I understood the meaning and the cause of all the mysterious happenings.

I finally reeled in a 200-pound loggerhead turtle close enough to the boat for me to release.

Vincenzo Manuppello
Myrtle Beach, South Carolina

Lots of Luck

My ocean fishing trip started out with the only mate on board getting sick and going to the hospital. We were fishing for sea bass, which usually run about 2 to 4 pounds. As luck would have it, my first two catches were sand sharks, about 8 to 10 pounds. My third catch was a 10-pound fluke. I had to hold him below water until the skipper ran down from the upper cabin to get a large net. Believe it or not, one scoop and we had the fluke. Talk about skill and absolute luck. Wow!

Frank Marano
Flushing, New York

Memories of a Good Friend

Years ago, when I was 6 years old, my mother and I moved from New Hampshire to Florida. I thought at the time it would be great, but once we were settled in Florida, I was very lonely, had no friends and wasn't doing very well in elementary school.

My mother worked all the time to support us, so on weekends I was left with the next-door-neighbor lady who watched me.

One day, sitting outside the house and feeling lonely, I heard this voice from across the street, "Young man, why aren't you out playing on such a beautiful day?" I yelled back that I had no friends here in Florida and that I was missing my friends back home. The gentleman came over and sat down next to me and was telling me a story of when he and his parents first moved to Florida, how he knew how I felt. He asked if I liked to go fishing, which I loved since the age of 3. I jumped up and said, "Let's go!" He said, tomorrow, if it was all right with my mother. She came home and I rushed her right over to that guy's house to meet him and his wife.

Well, his name was Duke and from that day on we fished every weekend we had a chance. Crabbing for blue crabs, fishing for red fish, snook, trout and anything else that would bite. For 4 years we were inseparable. Every weekend was someplace different. He loved to fish as much as I did and God, didn't I love it.

A couple of years later Duke passed away. His wife said that I made an unhappy retired old man very happy to have somebody to go fishing with. From that day on I have always tried to take somebody new that's never been fishing before out for at least one enjoyable day on the water.

Duke taught me so much; I'm very proud to have known him and to have fished with him!

Steve Davis
Sanbornton, New Hampshire